The Fifth Horseman of the Apocalypse

The Fifth Horseman of the Apocalypse

Studies in the Book of the Revelation

Jesse M. Hendley

Foreword by Jerry Vines

Radio Evangelistic Publications

By the same author:

Let's Go Right Now!
Five messages on Walking With God

How To Get Out of This World Alive!
Seven messages on Preparing for Eternity

Available from
Radio Evangelistic Publications
P.O. Box 90505
Atlanta, Georgia 30364

The Fifth Horseman of the Apocalypse
by Jesse M. Hendley
Copyright © 1985 by Jesse M. Hendley

Printed in the United States of America

Contents

6   **Contents**

To my wife Louise, for her unfailing encouragement,

To my staff and other faithful friends who have
helped in this joyful labor of love
but wish to remain anonymous,

With praise to the Father, the Son, and the Holy Spirit,

I gratefully dedicate this book.

Foreword

I am so thrilled that Dr. Hendley is putting into print his Bible studies through the Revelation. I have long regarded him as one of the finest Bible scholars, teachers, and evangelists of our day. God has used him in a miraculous way to win literally thousands of souls to the Lord. These messages from Dr. Hendley's pen and heart will bless you. I commend them to you.

I pray that the Lord will make it possible for many more Bible studies from Dr. Hendley's compassionate heart to be published. You will find these messages storehouses of Bible information.

Jerry Vines, Pastor

First Baptist Church
Jacksonville, Florida

Introduction

The Book of the Revelation was written by the beloved apostle John, the one who leaned on Jesus'
breast. It is interesting that God gave also the
Epistles—First, Second, and Third John—through
him. These he wrote first. They deal with the joy of fellowship in the church of the Lord Jesus Christ. The
Gospel of John was written later, about A.D. 85. It has
been called the greatest book in the world. I think the
Book of the Revelation would challenge that, but they
are certainly two of the greatest books.

The last book of the Bible, the capstone of it all, this
Book of the Revelation, was written about A.D. 95 or 96.
An old man now, John was on the Isle of Patmos,
banished there by Domitian, the Caesar of his day. Tradition tells us he worked in the mines. And there on
that island, on one tremendous Sunday, God gave him
this marvelous, enormous vision of the endtime, an unveiling known as "the Apocalypse."

How wonderful it is that we have this book today, so
that our generation may know what God said to John!
I like to think of it as a movie. Scene after scene unfolds
before our eyes. At one point, coming onto the stage of
this world, one after the other, will be the four horsemen of the Apocalypse. But the *Fifth Horseman* domi-
nates the entire book!

I hope that you have your Bible so that you may follow verse by verse as we go along. As you read, imagine that you are in the audience to whom these studies were delivered.

Chapter 1

The Revelation of Jesus Christ

The Central Theme

The theme of the book is the revelation of Jesus Christ. It is about Him; it is His book. We'll be reading also about the Antichrist, about the outpouring of God's judgments, about trumpets, monsters, and many other things. But don't let them distract you from the central person and theme, Jesus Christ.

Verse 1 begins, **"The Revelation of Jesus Christ."** The word translated "revelation" is from the Greek word *apokalupsis,* which means "to take off the veil, a disclosure of something we would not know otherwise." God has given us this tremendous *unveiling* of Jesus Christ! Sometimes when I think about Him or when we sing about Him, tears come to my eyes. Anyone who knows what salvation is loves Jesus! The very mention of His name is an overwhelming joy to the heart. God, who loves us even as He loves His Son, has given us this immense disclosure of His future plans concerning Jesus Christ.

Outline

The book can be outlined under three simple headings: Jesus Christ and His CHURCH, Jesus Christ and His KINGDOM, and Jesus Christ and His GLORY. The revelation concerning His church is found in chapters 1 through 3; His kingdom, chapters 4 through 19; His glory, chapters 20 through 22.

In chapters 4 and 5, beginning the long section on the Kingdom, the Father sits on the throne and has in His right hand the Book of the End, the Book of the Consummation. Jesus the Lamb walks up and takes that book out of the Father's hand and begins to tear open the seals. That ushers in the Seal Judgments. After that come the Trumpet Judgments. Then the Bowl Judgments. That leads to the climactic Second Coming of our Lord to earth. Then the Millennium. Then the final rebellion, when Satan is conquered. Then the destruction of the heavens and the earth. Then the creation of the new heavens and the new earth wherein dwells nothing but righteousness — Paradise Restored!

Source of the Book

The source of the Revelation is God. God gave it to Jesus: "**. . . to show unto His servants things which must shortly come to pass; and He sent and signified it by His angel unto His servant John**" (1:1). Notice that five terms are used here: God, Jesus Christ, an angel, John, and His servants. "Servants" refers to believers on the Lord Jesus Christ.

The source of the book is GOD. I tremble when I hear people talking adversely about this book, or speaking in ridicule about any portion of God's Word. To disbelieve what God has said is a terrible sin. God intends for His Word to be believed! Yet today there is much unbelief. Constant attempts are made to discredit the Bible. The reason is the rebellion in the human heart. Unbelievers want to cast God and His Word out of their lives so that they can live in their own sinful ways. God's Word and sin are incompatible. Yet some people claim to be Christians while living in sin.

One of the most prevalent sins today is homosexuality. I hate to sully your mind, but this illustrates my point. Recently on a talk show on television a man was talking about homosexuals. He said, "I am a Baptist preacher, and I am a homosexual. I couldn't disclose this at first because of the shame it would bring, but I am married to a man." The interrogator said, "What word do you have for your fellow homosexuals out there listening in?" He said, "I would say, take Jesus Christ as your authority to take away all shame and all sting regarding this."

I sat there in utter astonishment at the length to which some people will go, trying to defend or justify their sin! There is no defense. The Lord Jesus never condoned sin! Christ bore witness that the entire Bible is the Word of God, often quoting from the Old Testament, and nowhere is this sin of homosexuality condemned more vehemently than in Genesis. God rained down fire and brimstone on the cities of Sodom and Gomorrah because of this very sin. God burned those cities to the ground! And Jude in his epistle said that it was written in the book *as a warning* to future generations who would indulge in the same immorality. Sodom and Gomorrah are set forth as an example of suffering the vengeance of eternal fire. That's why my heart aches for these people. God's Word says that they who indulge in such sins, people who are without Christ, will go to *eternal fire.* That is what God says; I didn't say it. And if God destroyed Sodom and Gomorrah for this very sin, He is not going to spare people today. I repeat, Jesus bore witness to all of the Scriptures being the Word of God. It is said here again in the Revelation that it was God who gave this Book!

To Servants

"Which God gave to Him [Jesus] to show unto His servants" (v. 1). "Servants" is an interesting word in the Greek text. A Christian is called not just a servant but a slave. This Greek word *doulos* means "a bond-slave, a man in bonds to his master, a man who has no will of his own, a person who is wholly the property of another, one whose life and liberty and property are

under someone else's control." Someone may come and
work in your home for a certain time and leave at a certain time and be paid a certain amount, but that person
is not a slave. A slave has an owner. Here Christians
are called "bondslaves" of the Lord Jesus Christ, but
there is absolutely no shame or degradation implied, as
is usually associated with the word "slavery." John
uses the term simply to emphasize the fact that we are
not our own, that we belong to the Lord, that we are
bought with a price, the blood of our Master and
Savior! I am disturbed when I hear people say, "My
body belongs to me. I can do as I please with it." No,
friends. My body does not belong to me, and yours does
not belong to you, if you are a Christian. We belong to
the Lord Jesus Christ by right of creation and by right
of redemption. We are NOT our own! God bought us
with the terrible price of the blood of His Son.

Every time I think of that word "slave," I am reminded of Old Testament times. If a Hebrew man was without possessions, he would go into bondage to another
Hebrew man. But at a particular time, the Year of Jubi-
lee (the 50th year), slaves had to be set free. If a slave
had learned to love his master and didn't want to be
free, it was not compulsory or mandatory. There would
be a ceremony in which the master would bore a hole in
the lobe of his ear with an awl. That hole in the ear
marked him for life as being a slave owned by a master,
indicating that he did not want to go free. That mark
said, "I love my master. I'd rather be a slave to my good
master than to be free and on my own." That is how a
child of God feels about Jesus. What a Master! What a
Master is the Lord Jesus Christ!

So this book was written to "bondslaves" of Jesus
Christ. Every true Christian is a purchased, owned
slave of God and of the Lord Jesus. We are to have no
will of our own. Our will is to do God's will, even as
Jesus Himself said, *"I came not to do My will, but the will
of Him that sent Me."* He said, *"As the Father hath sent
Me, so send I you."* So our will is to do His will. We have
called attention to the fact that some people live in sin

and justify themselves, even claiming to serve the Lord. But the Bible says, *"Let all who name the name of Christ depart from iniquity"!* (II Timothy 2:19).

I repeat: the source of the Revelation is God. It came from Him; He sent it. I tremble sometimes about this matter of the inspiration of Scripture. In the Gospel of Matthew, Jesus said to Satan at the temptation, *"Man shall not live by bread alone, but by every word that proceedeth out of the mouth of God."* Notice that word "mouth." God has spoken! The Bible not only *contains* His Word; the entire Book *is* His Word. If it isn't, then we are wasting our time. I've wasted my life, and you are wasting your time in church. But this Bible IS the Word of God! And this Revelation is part of it.

Notice how God delivered it. He gave it to His Son Jesus, then Jesus gave it to an angel, then the angel gave it to John the Apostle on the Isle of Patmos. The entire endtime was revealed in one glorious day. How would you like to have been John on that particular day? Then John gave it to us who are bondslaves of the Lord Jesus.

Things to Come

". . . things which must shortly come to pass" (v. 1). The word "shortly" must be understood from the eternal viewpoint, God's viewpoint. With God, a day is as a thousand years and a thousand years as a day. God deals in eternalities. More than 1900 years have passed since the Revelation was written, and the fulfillment has not yet taken place. But it will come. God is moving in history, and when He begins to move toward the finish, He will move with rapidity.

What "things" are spoken of here? Things that are His. Things concerning the Lord Jesus. In John 13 we read that Jesus "loved His own who were in the world, and He loved them to the end," to the uttermost, endlessly. In those last chapters (13 through 21), we read of things concerning His own, His intimates, those who belong to Him. That is what we have here. Jesus committed to His servant John this precious revelation of things concerning Himself and His own.

Verse 2 tells us what is in this book. **"John bore record of the Word of God, and of the testimony of Jesus Christ, and of all things that he saw."** The content of the book is given here at the very outset. It is the Word of God and the testimony of Jesus Christ. The name "Jesus" means "Savior," and the title "Christ" means "God's Anointed One," the One appointed to bring this world out of the mess that man caused through his disobedience to God.

We have here *"the Word of God and the testimony of Jesus Christ."* Yet I have heard men stand in the pulpit—theologians who are teachers and preachers—speaking lightly and negatively of the Revelation. God has something to say about anybody who casts a shadow over it! (22:18,19). We are dealing with God and Christ in this book. Let us be careful what we say about it.

Readers, Hearers, Keepers

Next, notice the pronouncement of blessedness upon the readers, hearers, and keepers of this book. **"Blessed is he who keeps on reading aloud, and they who keep on hearing the word of this prophecy, and keep on keeping in their hearts the things which are written therein"** (v. 3). That is a free translation; each of those verbs has continuous action in the Greek.

There is blessing on the reader, which means the pastor in the pulpit who reads the book to his people and teaches them. This Revelation was sent to seven churches, and each preacher was to stand up and read this Revelation and expound it to his people, that they might be blessed of God.

In addition, the people were to "keep on hearing" the words of this book. We must not let it get away from us. We are to keep on hearing it, getting it into our minds and hearts.

Then too, we are to "keep" those things written therein. Keeping them has to do with living daily in the light of its profound truths. For he who has the hope of seeing Jesus Christ is continually purifying himself, even as Christ is pure. If we are looking forward to the return of Christ and the things of the endtime, we will be seeking to live honestly and earnestly day by day in the light of God's Word and of the fact that we will soon meet Jesus.

Salutation

In verses 4 through 8, we have John's salutation to the church: **"John to the seven churches."** At the very outset, he speaks to believers: **"Grace be unto you and peace."**

Grace! As the years go by, I find the word "grace" increasingly precious to my heart. Grace has to do entirely with God's Word. It includes the entire scope of salvation and Christian living. It is all of God and all of grace! You and I have just one thing to do, and that is *to believe God. "This is the work of God, that you believe"* (John 6:29). Someone came to Jesus and said, "What can we do to work the works of Him who sent You? What kind of work can we do to please God?" Jesus answered, "This is the work of God, that you *believe* on Him whom He hath sent." Only out of true belief will come action that is worth anything at all. Any service that does not come out of believing God and Christ is worthless. So the work of God is that people believe in God and Christ.

"Grace to you." "Grace" means "God's free, full, complete, unmerited forgiveness of sin, deliverance from every danger that is the consequence of the fall of man, and deliverance from sin in our personal lives." God has graciously forgiven all the sins of my entire life and will deliver me from all danger and bondage incurred because of the fall of man.

Now that results in *"peace."* No one has true spiritual peace until he knows his sins are forgiven. But if you believe God's Word that on the cross of Calvary He laid over on Jesus all the sins of your life and their consequences, all your sins from the cradle to heaven, the result is peace!

Grace and peace from whom? From the divine Trinity. **"From Him who is, and was, and is to** come." That is God the Father. **"And from the seven Spirits which are before the throne."** That is God the Holy Spirit. **"And from Jesus Christ."** That is God the Son.

God the Father is the One continually BEING. I want to pause here and mention God's name, YAHWEH, because the root of this name is the same as "the Being One," the One who has continual being. He was, and is, and is to come. He is always coming — continuous action. In every generation He comes continually.

The tenses of these three Greek verbs about God the Father add up to His eternality. That is the very meaning of the word YAHWEH, translated "LORD" (all capital letters) in the Old Testament. The LORD is my Shepherd; YAHWEH is my Shepherd, the Eternal One who had no beginning and will have no end is my Shepherd. From everlasting to everlasting HE IS GOD! Think back as far as you can, and you still have God. Think ahead as far as you can, and you still have God. He had no beginning, and He will have no end. You and I had a beginning. But, hear me, you and I will have no end! We'll live as long as God lives! One of the most profound truths that can come to the human mind is that we are going to live as long as God lives. Everyone who has ever lived is *alive* right now, and will continue to be alive throughout the ages of eternity, either in heaven or hell. That is the teaching of the Bible. When God creates a soul, that soul is created to exist as long as God exists. I can prove that from the language of the New Testament.

We read here of *"the seven Spirits which are before the throne."* I have labored over this expression for years, but I cannot understand why the Holy Spirit would be called here the "seven Spirits" of God. This has puzzled expositors. Some men believe there are actually seven Spirits. But if we examine all the phrases that are used relative to the seven Spirits, they all add up to One, the third member of the Trinity. This divine Being, the Holy Spirit, is seen elsewhere in the Bible in His sevenfold operation. For example, Isaiah 11:2, which I will not expound to you now, refers to the Holy Spirit.

"And from Jesus Christ." There are three divine Beings who look after us day and night. Many people think only of God the Father. Others think only of Jesus Christ. Others think only of the Holy Spirit. Seldom are all three persons given the worship due them. We read of the love of God in 1 John 4, and we read of the love of Jesus in John 13:1. But have we read of the love of the Spirit in Romans 15:30? The love of the Spirit! Only a person can love. An "it" cannot love. An "influence" cannot love. God the Father is a person, God the Son is a person, and God the Spirit is a person.

Someone may ask, "Isn't there just one God?" Yes. Jesus said, *"The Father and I are one."* That little word "one" means one in essence, not person. For Jesus said, *"The Father is greater than I."* There are three distinct persons in the Godhead, and yet they are One in essence. Genesis 1:1 says, *"In the beginning Gods [plural] created the heavens and the earth."* It is a plural noun, *Elohim.* A little later we read, *"Let US make man in OUR image and after OUR likeness"* (v. 26). To whom was God speaking? Not to an inferior being, such as an angel. He was talking to another divine Being. When Jesus was baptized, the heavens were opened and a voice was heard saying, *"This is My beloved Son in whom I am well pleased,"* and the Holy Spirit came down upon Him in the form of a dove. The Holy Trinity was there, three divine Beings.

In Psalm 110, David says, *"The LORD [YAHWEH] said unto my Lord [Adonai], Sit Thou at My right hand till I make Thine enemies the footstool of Thy feet."* The two Hebrew words translated "LORD" and "Lord" are veiled to most English readers. There are two Gods in that verse. God the Father is saying to God the Son, "Come up here and sit down at My right hand." When Jesus was crucified, men said, "Away with Him, crucify Him! We don't want Him! We'll run Him off the earth!" God said, "All right. You just come up here, Son, and sit at My right hand. Someday I will make those enemies of Yours the footstool for Your feet."

All three Persons of the Trinity were involved in creation, in redemption, and in the resurrection of Christ. And in the Book of the Revelation we find both God and the Lamb sitting on the throne. The Holy Spirit also is mentioned many times. So there are three divine Beings, and how blessed it is to realize that all three live in my heart since I believed on Jesus! If you read John 14, you will find that the Father, Son, and Spirit all dwell in the heart of the born-again believer. How can we ever be lost with the eternal Godhead looking after us!

Jesus Christ

Now let's look at Jesus Christ in verses 5 and 6: what He is, what He did for us, and what He will do for the world. What He is, first of all. **"Jesus Christ is the faithful witness, and the first-begotten of the dead, and the prince of the kings of the earth"** (v. 5). When Jesus Christ, *the faithful witness,* came to this earth, He revealed God the Father to us. You and I could not know God as our Father if it had not been for the faithful witness of Jesus Christ. Who teaches me that God is my Father, other than the Lord Jesus Christ?

Then, He is the *first-begotten* of the dead. That doesn't mean He was born of the dead. That same phrase is used in Colossians 1:18, and it means that as the firstborn He has sovereign position before God. Christ is the sovereign Lord! In Jewish households, the firstborn had the first place before the father. So also Jesus is first, *prototokos,* before the Father.

He is also *the ruler* [translated "prince"] of the kings of the earth. Does that mean that Jesus is ruling over the earth now? If that were so, Atlanta would certainly be a different place, and so would all the rest of the world. But He IS ruling in the hearts of believers, and He does have all authority. Before He went back to heaven He said, *"All authority is given unto Me in heaven and on earth."* The rulership of the earth has been given to Him, but He has not assumed it yet. In chapters 4 and 5 of this book, He begins to assume that rulership. We'll see Him take over the judgments of this world and move through till He brings every enemy down beneath His feet. Then He will present the kingdom to God the Father and say, "Father, mission accomplished."

This Christ of ours, who died on Calvary's cross, is destined to rule the nations of earth. We read in Revelation 11:15, *"The kingdoms of this world are become the kingdoms of our Lord and of His Christ, and He shall reign forever and ever."* Earlier manuscripts translate it, "The kingdom of this world has become the kingdom of our Lord and of His Christ." Every time I quote that verse, Handel's great "Hallelujah Chorus" comes to mind. "King of Kings, and Lord of Lords, and He shall reign forever and ever!" Yes, Christ is the faithful witness, the first-begotten of the dead, and the ruler of the kings of earth.

Then we read what He did for us. **"Unto Him who loved us and loosed us from our sins in His own blood and made us kings and priests unto God His Father"** (v. 5). Jesus loved us, loosed us, and made us. A simple outline, but how profound! I know I am skimming over great truths, but I cannot present the whole panorama of the book unless I do.

Translate the word "loved" in the present tense, *"loveth us."* The earlier manuscripts have the present participle: "Unto Him who keeps on loving us." He keeps on! Nothing can keep Him from loving us. The Apostle Paul cried out at the end of Romans 8, *"Nothing shall be able to separate us from the love of God which is in Christ Jesus our Lord."* He LOVETH us! Any voice that says Jesus no longer loves us when we do wrong or when we fail is lying. It is the voice of our adversary the devil, and he is a liar. God says that Jesus' love for us is eternal.

Then, "He *loosed* us from our sins," which is the better reading. It means that He set us free. He loosed us from our sins at the cost of His blood. He laid down His life to set us free.

And then, "He *made* us kings and priests unto God and His Father." Kings! We don't look much like it now, but we believers are kings in the kingdom of our Lord Jesus Christ. We'll be coming to that later in the book. Priests! We are intercessors before the Lord on behalf of others.

In verse 7 we read what He will do: **"Behold, He cometh with clouds, and every eye shall see Him, and they also which pierced Him [that means the Jewish nation], and all kindreds of the earth [Gentiles] shall wail [beat the breast in grief] because of Him. Even so, Amen [Let it be]."**

The world now is largely oblivious to Jesus Christ and His claims, but the day is coming when men will wail and cry out, "We made the biggest mistake of our lives in turning away from Jesus Christ, the Son of God!" Today personalities in television, theater, and sports receive more honor and acclaim than Jesus Christ. It will not always be that way. Someday *"every knee shall bow and every tongue confess that Jesus Christ is Lord, to the glory of God the Father"* (Philippians 2:10). He will come again, *"and every eye will see Him"* (Revelation 1:7). He will come back to earth, touching down on the Mount of Olives, and everyone in the world will see Him. By television? That could be, but don't rule out the miraculous. When you say God, you say Miracle. Nothing is impossible with God.

Notice Jesus' words in verse 8, **"I am Alpha and Omega."** Alpha and Omega are the first and last letters of the Greek alphabet. You may have seen them in stained-glass church windows. They speak of His tremendous Deity: **"The beginning and the ending, saith the Lord, which is and which was and which is to come, the Almighty."** There is a debate among scholars whether this is Jesus or God the Father talking. But the same expression "I am Alpha and Omega" is used in 22:13, where it is unmistakably Jesus. I believe profoundly that this is Jesus Christ in verse 8, speaking of His almightiness. The word translated "Almighty" is from the Greek *pantokrator,* meaning "the One who holds everything in His grasp." Everything! It strongly carries with it the sense of all rule, almightiness.

Christ is almighty! He is God! He can walk on the waves. He can say to a tempest on the Sea of Galilee, "Be still," and the waves subside; they become muzzled. Our Lord Jesus Christ is God. He can stand at the tomb of a man who has been dead 4 days and say, "Lazarus, come forth," and he comes forth. (Someone has quaintly said that if He had not said, "Lazarus," the whole crowd would have come forth from the tombs.) Jesus is co-equal with God in power. By Him all things were made. He created the worlds! This universe is the work of Christ's hands (John 1:3 and Colossians 1:16). He is almighty! And He says to us, "I am capable of doing what I promised I would do for you."

John on the Isle of Patmos

In verse 9 we have John's explanation of how he received the Revelation. Some people argue about the inspiration of the Bible. I wish everybody would be born again before they discuss inspiration, because after that you don't doubt it. You just pick up the Bible and read it and you know it is inspired. An unsaved man doesn't know it, but a saved man does.

So John tells us how he was inspired to write this book. **"I John, who am also your brother and companion in tribulation, and in the kingdom and patience of Jesus Christ, was in the isle that is called Patmos, for the Word of God and for the testimony of Jesus Christ"** (v. 9). Patmos was a rough little island in the Aegean Sea. It is still there. A cave, tradition says, was the place where John received the Revelation.

Notice that John doesn't say, "I am an Apostle." He simply says, "I am your brother and companion sharing in three things: tribulation, the kingdom, and endurance in connection with Jesus Christ." I wonder how many people today would join the church if they were told they would have tribulation. Well, we will have it, if we walk with God. This world doesn't love God, nor the Lord Jesus, nor His people. Jesus Himself suffered trouble and persecution. New converts should know that they are not going to heaven on flowery beds of ease. The prophets didn't have it easy. The early church didn't have it easy. When the Apostle Paul got up in the morning, he always faced the possibility of being killed before evening. Study the Book of Acts and see if that man's life wasn't on the line every day because of his faith in Jesus. As Christians, beloved, most of us have it awfully easy. I don't know whether persecution is coming to the church; some people are predicting that. I know one thing: the early church had it. But they were in the kingdom of God and they had endurance. That word "patience" means "endurance." They endured every trial that Jesus intended for them to have. The Christian life is one of endurance. Jesus said, *"In the world you will have tribulation, but in Me, peace."*

John in the Spirit

Notice in verse 10 the condition of inspiration: **"I was in the Spirit on the Lord's Day."** In the Spirit, on a Sunday. When you read "the Day of the Lord" in the Bible, that does not mean Sunday; the Day of the Lord is the time of terrible judgment upon the earth. So do not confuse the Lord's Day with the Day of the Lord. The Lord's Day is Sunday, the day we commemorate the resurrection of Jesus. Sometimes on Sunday you hear men pray, "God, bless us on this Sabbath Day." When will Christians learn that we are not under Law but under Grace? The Book of Galatians makes that very plain. We are not under the old feast days at all. The Sabbath was Saturday, distinctly given to the Jewish people under Law. Sunday is the Lord's Day, commemorating the resurrection of the Lord Jesus. The early church met on Sunday, the first day of the week. We Christians are not under Jewish Law in any manner, not even under their Sabbath. To call the Lord's Day "the Sabbath" is to confound truth, and we ought not to confound truth. So it was on Sunday, the first day of the week, that John received this vision.

He says, *"I was in the Spirit."* That simply means, "I was completely overwhelmed by the Spirit of God." To illustrate this, suppose I had a big rubber ball taller than I am, and it was cut in half, and I stepped inside that rubber ball. Then I asked someone to put the top half over me. I'd be inside that ball. It would totally surround me. John was totally enveloped by the Spirit and under the total control of the Spirit as God inspired him to write this book. I believe with all my soul in divine inspiration. I don't understand it all, but I accept it. I've read some great books, but they cannot compare with this Bible. I've done a lot of reading in my life, and I tell you there's nothing like the Bible! Devotional books may be good, but they are weak compared to the Bible. The Bible is unique in its spiritual power! A born-again person knows instinctively that this Book is divinely inspired, and he loves it more than any other book in the world.

"And I heard behind me a great voice, as of a trumpet saying, I am Alpha and Omega" (vv. 10, 11). This is unquestionably the voice of Jesus, for in verse 13 John turns and sees "one like unto the Son of Man," and there he describes the vision of Jesus.

The Command

Jesus then says to John, **"What thou seest, write in a book"** (v. 11). He didn't say "John, go preach this." He said, "Write it in a book." In my study of divine inspiration, I have traced this expression through the Bible. God told Moses, "What I have told you, write in a book." God told Jeremiah, "What I have told you, write in a book." (That book was burned, and God said, "Write another one," and Jeremiah did.) Every book in the Bible is from God! In them we have God's thoughts, God's mind. Paul said, "I preach and teach with words which the Holy Ghost teaches." David said, "The Spirit of the Lord was in me and His Word was in my tongue," as he wrote those Psalms. If you pick up a Psalm when you are spiritually hungry, immediately your soul is satisfied; the Spirit of God wrote those words. Nobody can live on husks. We Christians feed on the Word of God and find nourishment for our souls.

Jesus said, **"Write it in a book and send it to the seven churches in Asia."** There were seven literal churches. Seven is the perfect number. We find these churches in chapters 2 and 3: Ephesus, Smyrna, Pergamum, Thyatira, Sardis, Philadelphia, and Laodicea. Each of them received a copy of the Revelation, sent to them by John.

Many years ago, nobody had a personal copy of the Bible such as you and I have. I don't know how many Bibles I have; I haven't counted them. I mark one up, then get another, mark it up, and get another. Wouldn't it be pitiful if we had to go to church to find a copy of the Bible and beg to read this Book of the Revelation? In the Dark Ages, people didn't have Bibles. The very few, precious, handwritten copies were chained in the church. If anyone wanted to read some promises of God, he had to go to the church, and perhaps line up and await his turn. I say that, beloved, to cause us to appreciate our Bibles more. What a tragedy it would be if suddenly our Bibles were taken away from us and we had not hidden God's Word in our hearts!

John's Vision of Christ

"And I turned to see the voice that spoke with me [that is, to see the person who had spoken]. And being turned, I saw seven golden lampstands" (v. 12). Not candlesticks, but lampstands. The lampstand held the lamp that had the light. This is a picture of the church, which holds the Light.

"And in the midst of the seven lampstands One like unto the Son of man" (v. 13). "The Son of man" was Christ's favorite expression when referring to Himself. It has to do with His relationship to man, to us. It is a term for a human being. We find it in Daniel 7:13. The phrase "Son of man" is a study in itself. Jesus was, and is, the Son of God; but He was constantly calling Himself "the Son of man." It is used some 80 times in the four Gospels where we find the chronological life of the Lord Jesus Christ. He uses that term to identify with you and me in our humanity, our weaknesses and failures. He relates to us as our Savior, our Redeemer!

Here in the Revelation, the Apostle John sees not the lowly, human Jesus, but Christ in His great majesty, **". . . clothed with a garment down to the foot and girt about the paps [breasts] with a golden girdle. His head and His hair were white like wool, as white as snow; His eyes were like a flame of fire, and His feet like unto fine brass [bronze], as if they burned in a furnace, and His voice like the sound of many waters. And He had in His right hand seven stars; and out of His mouth went a sharp two-edged sword. And His countenance [face] was as the sun shineth in his strength"** (vv. 13-16).

This was the vision John saw of his beloved Master Jesus! Notice, He is girded about the breasts with a golden girdle—gold being symbolic of the preciousness of Jesus. His head and His hairs were white like wool—white speaking of the purity of Jesus. His eyes were as a flame of fire—the intelligence of Jesus! (Can you imagine the intelligence, the I.Q. of the Lord Jesus Christ?) His feet were like unto fine brass as if they had burned in a furnace; brass speaks of judgment, all through the Word of God. His voice was like the sound of many waters—His authority! Jesus said, "All authority is given unto Me in heaven and in earth." He had in His right hand seven stars and out of His mouth went a sharp two-edged sword; the sword speaks of judgment. We are going to find Christ moving through judgment! People back off from that word. They don't like to hear about judgment.

But Christ is not only the Lamb of God; He is also a Lion! If we don't understand this, we will not understand the Bible nor God. God has a lamblike character and a lionlike character. God is love, but God is also holy; His holiness never violates His love, and His love never violates His holiness. We are reminded here that Christ was full of both grace and truth (John 1:14).

Both love and holiness were exemplified in His life, never the one at the expense of the other.

"And His face was as the sun shining in its strength." That refers to His majesty. This is not the gentle Christ of the four Gospels, where He is seen in love, grace, and mercy, giving His blood for sinners. This is the Christ who will come the second time as the Judge of this world. He is going to clean up this mess! God gave Him the job of cleaning it up and He will not stop till He does it. He will right every wrong and make all things new and He will do it through judgment.

So tremendous was this sight of Christ that this man John, who was more intimate with Jesus than any of the disciples, fell at His feet as a dead man. He wrote, **"And He laid His right hand upon me, saying unto me, Fear not; I am the first and the last. I am He that liveth and was dead; and behold, I am alive forevermore, Amen; and have the keys of hell and of death"** (vv. 17,18). This majestic vision of Christ struck down the holiest man of his generation. It seemed to take the very life out of him, because he knew that horrible judgments were coming. A little later in the book we will find that there is silence in heaven for a period of 30 minutes before some of these horrible judgments strike the earth. Even heaven is aghast at the awful judgments God will have to bring upon men, in order to bring lasting peace to this earth.

The only way peace can come is for God to judge the non-peaceful people. If they resist and will not be converted, there is nothing left but judgment. Do you see God's problem? Think about that for a moment. Everybody cries out for peace. But how can there be peace when the majority of people don't want that which brings peace and are doing things the opposite of peace? They don't want God. They don't want to be converted. They won't change. There is nothing left but judgment, and God is going to bring it. Jesus is the One God has appointed to be the Judge of this earth. John fell at His feet as a dead man at this vision of Christ, His Master, coming in JUDGMENT!

John fell at His feet because fear had filled his heart. But Christ said, "Stop being afraid." "Stop being afraid" is also His word to us. If a child of God fears God, he need not fear anybody or anything else. Why?

First, it was Jesus Himself who said, *"Fear not."* In other words, "Since I am God, and you are trusting Me, don't be afraid. What have you to worry about?" Second, *"I am the first and the last."* Third, *"I am He that liveth and was dead."* The Greek says, "I became dead." Here it is not the usual verb *to be;* Jesus is saying, "I deliberately stepped into death." Jesus wasn't forced to go to the cross. He willingly laid down His life. He died in our place. Fourth, *"I am alive forevermore."* Fifth, *"I have the keys of hades and of death."* Our Lord has all authority!

Do you have problems? Isn't the Lord your Shepherd? Can't He take care of you? How long will He take care of us? Forever, "unto the ages of the ages," and that means eternally! Don't worry about being let down a week from now, or a month from now, or a year from now, or 10 years from now. He loves us with an everlasting love. He saved our souls from hell and our bodies from death. That is the meaning of "I have the keys of hell [hades, the unseen world] and of death [the grave]." In Luke 16 we read that the rich man died and was buried, "and in hell [hades] he lifted up his eyes, being in torment." He was a lost soul. Jesus gave His life to save our souls from death and the grave, and someday He will have a new body for us.

One day I had the funeral service of a woman greatly used of God in the early days of my Christian life, a blessing to me and to my wife. She had asked that I preach her funeral service. As I looked at her in her casket, I thought, Wouldn't it be tragic if we didn't have a Bible, if we didn't have a church where the Light of Christ was gleaming! I couldn't have walked into that funeral service if it were not for the Gospel of Jesus Christ! It gives the assurance of salvation for the soul and for a new body. How often we should say, "Thank You, Jesus, that You have the keys, the authority over death and hell, and that You have delivered our souls from the grave and will give us new bodies." There is coming a resurrection day, beloved. What a glorious hope! We owe it all to Jesus Christ.

Jesus said to him: **"Write the things which thou hast seen [the vision of Himself], and the things which are [Revelation 2 and 3, concerning the churches], and the things which shall be after these things"** (v. 19). That is, Revelation 4 through all the judgments to the new heavens and the new earth.

Churches and Pastors

"The mystery of the seven stars which thou sawest in My right hand and the seven golden lampstands. The seven stars are the angels of the seven churches" (v. 20). The Greek word *aggeloi,* "angels," is used of "messengers." This cannot mean anything other than the pastors of the churches. It is precious to know that Christ holds the pastors of the churches in His right hand. It is a profound truth.

"The seven candlesticks which thou sawest are the seven churches" (v. 20). Beloved, I want to impress upon you the authority of Christ in the church. It is awesome to read in Revelation 1 through 3 of Christ and His church. The greatest thing on this earth is the church of the Lord Jesus Christ, because it is His Bride. In Ephesians 5:25, Paul says, "Husbands, love your wives *as Christ loved the church and gave Himself for it."* Christ is going to present it to Himself *"a glorious church, not having spot, nor wrinkle, nor any such thing, but that it should be holy and without blemish."* Christ will take us unto Himself as His Bride!

Here He stands in the midst of the golden candlesticks. When Jesus came to this world, He said, *"I am the light of the world."* When He left, He said, *"Ye are the light of the world."* The church is to shine as a light to the world. If this light goes out, who will shine and give any hope in the darkness? When the church's light goes out, this world has no light. The only hope of this world is the hope brought through the church, given by the Lord Jesus Christ. Let's pray for our churches! Let's thank God if we belong to a church that is exalting and honoring the Lord Jesus.

The church, which is composed of Christians, is called the temple of God in 1 Corinthians 3:16. *"Know ye not that ye are the temple of God and the Spirit of God dwells in you? He that destroyeth the temple of God, him will God destroy."* Whenever I find someone hurting the church, I want to say, "Brother, did you know that God destroys those who destroy His church?" It is the only light this world has. If you take the Gospel out of this world, the world is plunged into utter darkness and men have no hope whatsoever.

The church has been bought by the Lord Jesus Christ. Paul said to the elders at Ephesus, *"Remember the church, which Christ purchased with His own blood."* Jesus is the unseen Head of the church, and also the Savior of the body.

He says the pastor is a gift to the church. A pastor is in a unique position. When Christ ascended on high, *"He gave some apostles [they are gone], some prophets [I don't believe we have prophets today], some evangelists [we do have evangelists today], and some pastors [that means shepherds, who look after the flock], and teachers [those who teach God's Word with authority]."* The pastor is a shepherd of the flock under Christ, who is the unseen Shepherd. This is not said of anyone else. He is also the teacher. He is a pastor-teacher in the assembly. He is also called the ruler of the church. *"Obey them that have the rule over you, and submit yourselves, for they watch for your souls as they that must give account"* (Hebrews 13:17). God didn't say that other men are to watch for your souls and must give account for the souls in the church. We may have men in the church who are very brilliant in their field, men of all types of professions and occupations and trades. They can help in their way, and if they do it in Christ's name, they will receive a reward. *"Those who receive a prophet in the name of a prophet shall receive a prophet's reward"* (Matthew 10:41).

Some churches are getting rid of their faithful pastors. I know of a church that recently dismissed its pastor, a godly man. They do not realize what they have done. God says, "He that destroys the temple of God, him will God destroy." I know a woman whose life was snuffed out after taking a stand against her pastor. The church had a prayer meeting where the people prayed, "Lord, remove every obstacle." The preacher and his wife prayed, "Even if it means moving us." A few days later this woman's house caught on fire. An invalid in one of the rooms somehow managed to escape, and a canary escaped, but this woman's life was snuffed out. I tell you, friends, we should be careful what we say about a God-called, God-anointed, Spirit-filled pastor. He is God's man, a gift from God, the shepherd of the flock, a teacher of His Word, and the spiritual ruler, and members are to obey his teaching. He is spiritually responsible for their souls. He must give an account to the Lord.

The deacons are called to help the pastor do the Lord's work. I have found churches up and down the land where deacons had the mistaken idea that they were supposed to rule the pastor and the church. That isn't true, yet it is a common thing today. You'd be surprised how many pastors have asked me to bring this Bible truth to their churches. A godly man who faithfully preaches the Word stands in Christ's stead; and as he teaches God's Word, his word is to be obeyed.

Beloved, I repeat, the greatest thing in this world is the church of the Lord Jesus Christ. He is "in the midst of the lampstands." He holds the preachers in His right hand. And if we want the blessings of God in any church, we must recognize God's order of authority. Christ is the unseen Head, and the pastor is the seen head. The deacons are to help. The musicians are to help. The teachers are to help. But all of these can never take the place of the pastor, who has a unique position of leadership and responsibility before God.

I remember when I went to a church as a young preacher. I had seen a man die in his sins. I saw a vision of this lost world one night in prayer. I began to preach evangelistic messages. But some of the church people didn't want that. I didn't realize the opposition that was going on in the church; I was just following the Holy Spirit's leading. One Sunday afternoon I went down to the church for a meeting, and three of my leading men got up and left—the chairman of the board of deacons, the Sunday School superintendent, and another leader. They walked right out. It was a small church in those days, before the growth began. I felt hurt, and I went home crying (my wife will tell you). I walked into our home and said, in the words of Jacob, "These things are against me." She didn't know what I was talking about. I said, "Three man have just left. They walked out and left me flat." She looked at me and said, "God has just gotten them out of your way. He will give you some other men in their place." You know, that is just what God did. And that was the beginning of a 14-year-long revival, 14 years of *the greatest blessings of God* my eyes have ever seen in my long ministry. God gave me deacons to do the job.

Now I pause here to say something solemnly. Those three men missed God's best. They didn't understand. They didn't believe that I was called of God, that the Holy Spirit was upon me, that God's anointing was upon me, that God was leading me as the pastor of that church. They resisted God's leading. They didn't know what I have just been trying to tell you about the pastor's unique position in the church, that God has given him the red line to His throne concerning the church. If a pastor is a God-called, Spirit-filled, Spirit-anointed man, faithfully standing with God's Word, a man of prayer, a man who loves souls, and he preaches the Word to the people, God says the people of the church are to obey him and submit to his leadership.

Chapter 2

Messages From Christ
(Ephesus, Smyrna, Pergamum, Thyatira)

Letters to the Seven Churches

In chapter 2 we come to the letters Jesus sends to the seven churches. He gives them to John. Our Lord is alive in the midst of the churches, and He will be in the midst of them right on through to glory. Jesus said, *"Where two or three are gathered together in My name, there am I in the midst."* He is continually present. In our assemblies, Jesus is present, and He speaks to us through His Word.

Remember that these were seven literal letters to seven literal churches, most of which were only 30 to 50 miles apart. You can visit the sites of those cities today.

There is another truth here. Many Bible students believe that these seven churches are a picture of the seven stages in the progression of church history, from the early church down to the apostasy that will prevail just before Christ comes in the Rapture.

I'd like to remind you that they are also for us today. Jesus said in verse 7, **"He that hath an ear, let him hear."** This means, "If you are capable of hearing, if you are born again and in touch with Me so that you can understand spiritual truth, then hear what the

Spirit is continually saying to the churches." "What the Spirit saith" should be translated "What the Spirit is continually saying," because the verb is in the present tense, continuous action. The Spirit of God is still constantly speaking to the churches today.

One great student of the Bible, a commentator and a Greek scholar, has said that one of the most important things Christians can do is to study these letters to the churches, because if we studied and obeyed them they would unquestionably bring revival. Another great man of God has said that in these days we need the warning of Jeremiah, who thundered out against backslidden Israel, and that we need also the warnings found in this Book of the Revelation, chapters 2 and 3, where the Lord speaks to the churches. Jesus walks up and down in the midst and observes what is going on, and John writes of His attitude toward those things.

We will go through these letters quickly. Notice that usually in each letter the Lord first gives John the command to write. Then there is a description of Himself.

He commends what He can and condemns what He must. Remember that our Lord is Truth. Nothing can ever make Him deviate from the truth. When He paints a picture of a church, that's the way it is. Whenever I speak to young people, I remind them that they have asked me to "tell it like it is." But when I do tell it like it is, they sometimes tune me out because they don't really want the truth.

Friends, our Lord is going to say some things in this book that we may not like. Just remember, it is the truth. The Bible is a tough book. It isn't easy reading. Oh, you can pick out a little sweet thing here, and skip over and pick out another little sweet thing there, but that is not studying the Bible. If you study right through the Bible and let God speak to you, you will find some rough things. But the person who really loves God will face the truth as it is. That is the only way to be blessed, friends. There is no other way. So our Lord gives commendation and condemnation.

He also gives advice. He goes beyond in many instances and gives commands. Then He gives warnings of judgment. I remind you, this is not the sweet-and-kind Jesus that unbelievers have imagined in their own minds. Beloved, we must face the facts concerning who Jesus is and what He is like. Study the New Testament. Face the truth. He didn't always say the sweet things. Our blessed Lord said some of the most cutting, biting, blistering things that have ever fallen on human ears. He had a reason for it. Our Lord always told the truth! He spoke the truth in love.

Then at the close of each letter you find a promise to the overcomer.

Ephesus (2:1-7)

Let's begin now with verse 1. The first letter is to the church at Ephesus. **"Unto the angel of the church of Ephesus write."** This is Jesus' command to John to write to the preacher of the church at Ephesus.

Next is the description of Himself. **"These things saith He that holdeth the seven stars [pastors] in His right hand, and who walketh in the midst of the seven golden candlesticks."** Our Lord walks in the midst of the churches. He knows exactly what is going on all the time in the churches, those seven early churches and our churches today.

Then He commends them: **"I know thy works, and thy labor, and thy patience [endurance, enduring that which opposes you], and how thou canst not bear them which are evil, and thou hast tried [tested] them who say they are apostles and are not, and hast found them liars. And hast borne [endured, carried the heat of the day], and hast patience [endurance, perseverance] and for My name's sake hast labored and hast not fainted"** (vv. 2,3). Our Lord looked first at the good things they had done and commended them. The early church was not perfect. There was evil and wrong in the church from the very beginning. The church has never been perfect, but it will be someday. The Lord will present to Himself a glorious church, not having spot nor wrinkle.

He commended them for their labor. "I know thy

works, and thy labor." He mentions their endurance,
and how they tested people who claimed to be apostles
but were not. Notice that there were false professions
in that day. The church is not perfect because people
are not perfect and will not be until they get to heaven.
Even one of the original Twelve, Judas Iscariot, was a
betrayer of the Lord. Our Lord commends what He can,
but then He must condemn.

"Nevertheless I have somewhat against thee"
(v. 4). Jesus said, "Brother Pastor and church people, I
have something against you. You have left your first
love." What was it in that church that displeased the
Lord Jesus Christ? They had left their first love. What
is "first love"? Paul tells us in I Corinthians 13 that if
we don't have love we are zero, absolutely nothing.
That chapter is one of the most convicting chapters in
the Bible. *"If I speak with the tongues of men and of
angels, and have not love, I am as a sounding brass or a
clanging cymbal."* I am just a lot of noise, that's all. I
can work my fingers to the bone and give my body to be
burned, but it is zero if I don't have love.

There are three loves in the Bible: Love to God, love
to fellow Christians, and love to this lost world. The
first is to God Himself. The church at Ephesus began to
slip in their love for the Lord Himself! Beloved, when
our love for the Lord goes, our service cannot be what it
should be toward Christians and this lost world. Without this First Love, we dry up and are not what we
ought to be. Our Lord wants a loving church. A loveless
church is a tragic thing. Whenever I hear someone say
they love a human being more than God, I shudder, because the first and greatest command of God is *"Thou
shalt love the Lord thy God with all thy heart."* That
means with all your affection, with all your mental
power, with all your strength, with all your physical
being. After that, *"Love thy neighbor as thyself."* God
must be Number One! If I do not love the Lord in my
heart, if I have let slip my communion with Him, my
service is not acceptable to Him. We are not to let our
First Love diminish. The Lord knows when we do, and

He is not going to let us get by with it. If we slip in our fellowship with Him, He will make us restless until we get back in touch with Him again.

LOVE is what He is talking about here. I don't know any portion of the Bible that presents more clearly love and works in the proper proportion than we find it in these two chapters. Love must come first, then service. Because without love, service equals zero in the eyes of God. The psalmist said, *"I love Thee, O Lord, my strength! Whom have I in heaven but Thee? There is none upon earth that I desire besides Thee."* David was saying, "When I go to heaven, I won't find anyone like You, Lord. You are Number One. You are beautiful beyond words. I love people here on earth, but they are nothing compared with You." *"As the hart panteth after the waterbrook, so panteth my soul after Thee, O God!"*

Love comes first. Suppose I say, "I want to go out and work for You, Jesus." He will say, "Let's have a little time together first." Fellowship, our personal relationship with Him, comes first.

I was in a certain city one day, sitting with the pastor of one of the greatest churches in the Southland, a church that led in the number of professions of faith and baptisms in that entire region. Then things began to change. They weren't winning as many souls. Ten years ago I had a meeting there and 150 souls came to the Lord in one week. But the people are not winning souls like that now and this has broken his heart. I was in this meeting with him and things were not going well. Souls were not coming to the Lord, as we had prayed for and had expected. On Saturday morning we had breakfast together and then went by the post office. When we went back to the car, we just sat there, we two preachers of the Word. After a silence, he looked at me and said, "Jess, I don't want the Lord to punish me." "My beloved brother," I said, "Jesus Christ is not interested first in what you do for Him. He is interested in you, your heart, your fellowship. He doesn't want you to be grieved and miserable and unhappy. He wants you to be happy in Him."

I felt that was what God wanted me to say to that dear brother. Every Christian needs to know that personal fellowship and communion with the Lord are far more important to Him than activity. Work will follow, if we maintain our private times with the Lord. The Lord doesn't want us to substitute work for worship and labor for love.

After being a pastor, God called me to evangelism, and for 14 years God gave revival after revival. Souls were being saved. The blessing was glorious. Then He put me into a church where there had been conflict and division, and the fighting was still going on. Of all people on earth to try to rebuild the foundation, the Lord picked me. At first I argued with Him about it. But He knows what He is doing and He sent me there. I stayed for 2 years and 3 months, and I think if I had stayed longer I would have died. My wife wanted to stay, but she knew I wouldn't live if I remained in that place. All I could do was try to rebuild the foundation. What can you do in a church where the people are at daggers' points with each other? They had actually written poison-pen letters to each other before I came. I got one of them, just one. Anyway, we put a stop to that practice. But other conditions continued and 80 of the leaders left the church. The funds dropped to $300, and you can't operate a church on $300. It was tragic. No one was winning souls. The only souls won for Christ were when I'd take a deacon with me and we would go out visiting in homes. We won a few people and baptized them. All through this situation I was crying to God. I thought the world had fallen in on me. I said, "Lord, what have I done? What has happened, that You would send me here, taking me out of evangelism where in meeting after meeting we saw Your glorious victories? Why am I down here in this barren place, in the midst of a broken church? Why, Lord? Why?"

Then the Lord said as plainly to me as I am standing here talking to you, "I want you to know, Jess Hendley, that I am more interested in your heart and your fellowship with Me than I am in your service, even your soul-winning." I learned a very important lesson. There will come a day when we won't be able to win any souls to Jesus, but our love-relationship with Christ will not stop. We'll still be having sweet fellowship and communion with Jesus. That difficult experience didn't mean that He was through with me. But He taught me that my fellowship with Him was far more important to Him than my service.

That was when I learned as never before how much the Lord loved me. Jesus was teaching me His personal love for me! He said, "Jess, I don't need you to win souls. I can make these stones cry out and preach the Gospel. I don't have to have your service. But I MUST have fellowship with you, We MUST stay in communion with each other." I had been maintaining a prayer life, but this experience deepened and strengthened it.

I hope you have learned this lesson, friends. A lot of people measure their joy by the fruit of their *work*. Not so. That is good, but it is not number one. If you use that as your measurement, the day will come when you will learn differently. You remember that Jesus sent 70 men forth to preach His Word. They came back rejoicing, saying, "Even the demons are subject to us in Your name." Jesus said, "Do not rejoice in demons being subject to you. Rejoice rather that your names are written in heaven. Don't rejoice in what you are doing for Me; rejoice in what I have done and am doing for you." We can never be satisfied with what we are doing for Him, but we can be satisfied with what He is doing for us.

Then He calls for repentance. **"Remember, therefore, from whence thou art fallen"** (v. 5). Here is a church filled with people who have let the love of the Lord, their communion with the Lord, their devotion to the Lord, their Bible study, their prayer, slip! Coolness has come over their heart and soul, but they are still going through the motions, the ritual of their church. The Lord calls it a fall. A fallen church! There are many fallen churches, friends, I'm sorry to say.

"Remember . . . and repent." Repentance means

getting back to where you were. Repentance is turning back to God after you have turned away from Him. **"Repent and do the first works, or else I will come quickly and remove the candlestick [lampstand] out of its place, except thou repent"** (v. 5).

There is a warning from Jesus. What does it mean to remove the candlestick? It means that the light will go out. Jesus is saying, "I will turn out the light." You will have a church that will just be going through the ritual, with no power and no blessing. In many of our churches the preacher preaches, and the singers sing, and the deacons "deac," and the teachers teach, but there is no love for God in it and no power in it. Why? Because God has turned off the light! Jesus has removed the candlestick out of its place. I know of a place here in Atlanta that 40 years ago was the center of evangelistic blessing. Today it's a warehouse. The light went out somewhere along the way. Our Lord said, "I will remove the candlestick if you don't repent and come back into intimate relationship and fellowship with Me. I will give the blessing to somebody else; they will receive the blessing."

Then the Lord said in verse 6, **"But this thou hast, that thou hatest the deeds of the Nicolaitans, which I also hate."** Jesus hating? Yes! To love is to hate. You cannot love without hating that which would destroy your love. The Lord said, "I hate the deeds of the Nicolaitans." Now, who they were we do not know. We do know that they taught false doctrine and the Lord hated it. He was saying, "When you hate what I hate, that is in your favor."

Then He closed with a message to the individual: **"He that hath an ear, let him hear what the Spirit is saying to the churches"** (v. 7). He that is born again, he that is capable of hearing, he that is in spiritual communion with Me so that he can tell what the Spirit is saying, let him hear! The Spirit of God is constantly telling us things, beloved, but either we don't have ears to hear or we don't take time to listen. The Lord can't reach us if we're not listening. People are not listening! If people would listen, there would be many more conversions to Christ.

When I was saved, I thought, "This is so wonderful! People don't know about this! I'm going to tell everybody I know, and they will fall all over themselves coming to Christ to be saved." You know what happened? Yes, you do. What the Lord is still saying to people is wonderful, but they will not listen! They don't have ears to hear. They are not capable of hearing what He has to say, nor what we have to say. I had to learn that as a preacher. People must listen, open their hearts, be born again, and be in right relationship to the Lord, to receive what the Spirit is saying to the churches. Today, in our generation, the Spirit is continually trying to speak to our churches. Blessed are they who have ears to hear!

Then the Lord gives this church a promise, but I will take that up later when I summarize all the promises to the churches.

Smyrna (2:8-11)

Now we come to the church in Smyrna. Jesus says to John: **"Unto the angel of the church in Smyrna write: These things saith the first and the last, which was dead and is alive [that is a description of Himself]; I know thy works"** (vv. 8,9). The Lord knows what we have done. Actually, nobody knows our works but the Lord. My wife knows a little about my work, and a few other friends know, but nobody except the Lord really knows how much I study or don't study His Word, how much I pray or don't pray, how much I work or don't work. He knows exactly how much time I put in for Him. He knows how much I honestly seek to please Him in prayer and Bible study, working and witnessing. He is keeping the books, and He has a book on you. He knows your works as an individual, and He knows the work of your church.

"I know thy works and tribulation," affliction, distress, suffering. Smyrna was a poor church. But Jesus added a paradoxical word: **"but thou art rich."** Our Lord here distinguishes between having material possessions and spiritual wealth. In Matthew 6:33, He says that if we seek first the Kingdom of God and His righteousness, all other things will be added to us. I have tried to live in the light of that promise for 48 years, and I know it's so.

"And I know the blasphemy of them which say they are Jews and are not, but are the synagogue of Satan" (v. 9). There were some people in Smyrna who claimed to be true Jews but were not. The word "Jew" comes from the word Judah, and Judah comes from the word in Hebrew which means "to praise." A true Jew was one who praised the Lord with his lips and with his life. These in Smyrna pretended to be honest Jews and worshipers of the Lord but were in reality a synagogue of Satan. Jesus is the Truth, and He cannot tolerate hypocrisy. He thunders out against pretense and play-acting. He sees behind the false front. He rips off the mask and reveals the truth. These men were His adversaries, pretending to be for Him when they were really against Him. One of the worst things that can happen to a church is for subversives to come into the camp and work subtly and insidiously on the inside to do their destructive work. I have seen it.

"Fear none of those things which thou shalt suffer" (v. 10). To a church in the midst of difficulty, poverty, and false profession, our Lord says, "Don't be afraid. Don't give up. Don't quit."

"Behold, the devil shall cast some of you into prison, that ye may be tried [tested, put to the test], and ye shall have tribulation [trouble] for ten days. Be thou faithful unto death, and I will give thee a crown of life" (v. 10). Someone may say, "The Lord tells these people that they will have trouble; I thought that when a person became a Christian, his trials were all over." No, that seems to be a common idea, but we don't get it from the New Testament. God's people in this world have always had trials, and we still have them. As long as the devil is the usurper of this world and the majority of people are not born again, how can there be anything else but trouble?

Our Lord says, **"Be faithful unto death."** Die rather than be unfaithful! Keep your faith in Me and your testimony for Me, even if it costs you your life. The martyrs of the church have done that, and are doing it in this generation in which we are living. There are people this very day who are dying for the name of Jesus. He will give them a crown of life!

The "ten days" here may refer to ten successive periods of persecution that were to come against Christians. They have been recorded by church historians. Notice that the early church had enemies. And the church today has enemies. We are in a hostile world, spiritually. The greatest conflict going on today is not nation against nation with armaments that kill physically; the greatest battle is the spiritual conflict between the forces of Christ and the forces of Satan!

Then the Lord gives them a promise, **"He that hath an ear, let him hear what the Spirit is saying to the churches."** Again, I want to gather up all the promises at the conclusion.

Pergamum (2:12-17)

Now we come to the letter to the church at Pergamum. Jesus tells John, **"To the angel [pastor] of the church at Pergamum write: These things saith He which hath the sharp sword with two edges."** That is a description of Himself. He gives a self-description in each of these letters. **"I know thy works."** Again He says this. He knew what was going on in that church. **"And where thou dwellest."** He knew where they lived. **"Even where Satan's throne is."** This church was carrying on God's work in the very shadow of the devil's throne. **"And thou holdest fast My name."** You grasp My name. **"And have not denied My faith, even in those days when Antipas was My faithful martyr, who was slain among you, where Satan dwelleth."** You see, He commends what He can. They held fast His name, had not denied the faith, had held steady even when one of them by the name of Antipas was martyred rather than be unfaithful to Christ and the Word.

I have often thought about martyrs for Christ, how they gave their lives, and I have wondered how I would stand up for the Lord Jesus Christ if my life were on the line. Would I be true to Him? I don't think I can answer that; I don't think you can either. These people made the choice, and they did so with the power the Lord gave them at the time. Just as He will give us dying grace when the time comes, so also He gave to those martyrs the dying grace they needed. Thousands of the early Christians were slaughtered, thrown to the lions, and suffered many forms of torture and death, choosing to be true to Jesus rather than deny His name. Every one of those martyrs could rise up and convict us when we today are untrue to Christ. How many of us, friends, would lay down our lives for Him, as they did?

Now notice verse 14. **"But I have a few things against thee."** They were doing well in some ways, but He wanted them to get rid of certain things that were hindering fruit-bearing. You remember His teaching in John 15 about fruit, more fruit, and much fruit. He wants the Father to be glorified. He Himself glorified the Father, and He wants us to glorify the Father. When we bear some fruit, He cleanses us that we might bear more fruit, and by bearing much fruit the Father is glorified.

What did He have against this church? Again, He commends what He can and rebukes what He must. He said: **"Thou hast there them that hold the doctrine of Balaam, who taught Balak to cast a stumbling-block before the children of Israel, to eat things sacrificed unto idols and to commit fornication"** (v. 14). When the children of Israel were coming out of the land of bondage and coming through Moab, Balak the king of Moab didn't like it and wanted the children of Israel to be cursed. So he went to a prophet named Balaam and said, "Curse for me the people of Israel." Balaam tried to do it, but God wouldn't let him. One of the greatest statements on grace in the entire Word of God is found in this account in Numbers 22, 23 and 24. Balaam did his level best to try to curse Israel, and he finally had to say, "How can I curse those whom God has not cursed?" They were, indeed, a crowd of complaining sinners, but God in His grace didn't charge Israel with perverseness and iniquity. The Lord God was with them. The shadow of the King was over them.

So Balaam said to Balak the king, "I'll tell you what to do. The way to get at God's people, since God will not let them be cursed, is to cause them to stumble and fall. Cause the women and the men to mingle and to commit fornication. This will provoke God's wrath, and He Himself will bring judgment upon them." He advised Balak to cast this stumblingblock before Israel: to commit fornication and idolatry which God hates. That was the doctrine that was in the church at Pergamum.

"So hast thou also them that hold the doctrine of the Nicolaitans, which thing I hate. Repent, or else I will come unto thee quickly and will fight against them with the sword of My mouth" (vv. 15,16). Repent! This is His command, and disobedience carries with it a threat. Our Lord Jesus died on the cross for us and loves us, but to the disobedient individual or church He will bring discipline. He will bring judgment where judgment is needed. I have observed this time and again in the ministry.

"He that hath an ear, let him hear what the Spirit is saying to the churches." Again, I pass up the promise until later.

Thyatira (2:18-29)

Now to the church at Thyatira. **"Unto the angel [pastor] of the church at Thyatira write: These things saith the Son of God, who hath His eyes like a flame of fire, and His feet like fine bronze. I know thy works, and love, and service, and faith, and thy patience [endurance] and thy works, and the last to be more than the first"** (vv. 18,19).

In other words, "I know what you are doing for Me and how much you pray. I know when you go out visiting for Me, and drive buses and teach the classes out of love for Me. I know what you are doing, pastor, when you study and pray and preach and work. I know, deacons, when you are faithful to help the pastor carry on My work. Notwithstanding, I have a few things against thee."

Here in verse 20 is the deserved rebuke, the condemnation: **"Thou sufferest [allowest] that woman Jezebel, who calleth herself a prophetess, to teach and to seduce My servants to commit fornication and to eat things sacrificed to idols."**

There was a certain woman in that church who reminded the Lord of Jezebel in the Old Testament. Jezebel was a wicked heathen queen, married to King Ahab. One day Ahab was moping around the palace, and she said, "What's wrong with you?" He replied, "I want Naboth's vineyard, and he won't sell it to me." She said, "You are the king! You can have anything you want," and she sent some wicked men to Naboth's house and had him murdered. One came back and said to her, "Naboth is dead. Come and get your vineyard." She and Ahab went down, and there was Naboth, killed, and dogs were licking his blood.

God then sent His prophet Elijah to them. Read it for yourself in I Kings 21:17-23. He shook his bony finger in the king's face and said, "Thus saith the Lord! In this very place where the dogs are licking the blood of Naboth, they are going to eat Jezebel's flesh." Friends, we had better believe what God says. Twenty years went by, and it looked as if that prophecy would never be fulfilled. But God's Word is always fulfilled. Second Kings 9:30 says that Jehu came and took over the kingdom. He drove up in his chariot to the palace. Jezebel stuck her head out of the second-story window and cried, "Zimri killed his master and got by. I don't have to reap what I've sown, do I?" And Jehu said to her attendants, "Throw her down!" They threw her down and her body landed with a thud on the pavement. Then Jehu drove his horses and chariot over her body and went inside the palace to eat. He said to the servants, "Go out there and take that cursed woman and bury her. After all, she is a king's daughter." But when they went out to pick up Jezebel's body, they

found only a few gnawed bones of hands and feet, ful-
filling the word of God that the dogs would eat the flesh
of Jezebel. Beloved, God doesn't always pay off on
Friday. But payday is coming. What God says will be,
will be. It will come.

Now here in the church of Thyatira was a woman
who was rebellious against God, yet she had tremendous influence. She was teaching God's people to
commit fornication (sexual vice), and to eat things
sacrificed to idols. It was the same kind of immorality
that was going on in the church at Pergamum. Jesus
said: **"I gave her space to repent of her fornication,
but she repented not. Behold, I will cast her into a
bed, and them that commit adultery with her into
great tribulation, except they repent of their
deeds"** (vv. 21,22). Except they repent! Jesus was
giving them one more chance. Oh, the grace of the Lord
Jesus Christ!

**"I will kill her children with death, and all the
churches shall know that I am He which searcheth
the reins [minds] and the heart, and I will give
every one of you according to your works"** (v. 23).
According to your faith? No, your works. Beloved, we
do wrong to emphasize faith and leave out works, or
emphasize works and leave out faith. They are both in
the New Testament. They go together; they are in-
separable. In this book our Lord speaks much about
works. Works come from faith.

Notice, He searches our thoughts and affections. He
knows our thoughts afar off (Psalm 139). The Lord
looks on the inside and desires truth in the inward part.
"In the hidden part," cried David, "make me to know
wisdom." God has x-ray eyes. He sees inside me. He
sees everything I am thinking as if it were on a television screen. He knows our every thought! We think
much about our outward life, but the Lord is more concerned with our inward life.

**"But unto you I say, and unto the rest in
Thyatira, as many as have not this doctrine
[teaching] and have not known the depths of**

Satan, as they speak, I will put upon you no other
burden" (v. 24). They went around boasting about
knowing the deep things of Satan, the adversary of
God. **"But that which you do have, hold fast till I
come"** (v. 25). They were a struggling church.

I was talking to a pastor who has been having a
struggle, a battle. He has had one problem after another for 10 years. I admire him so much because he has
been a faithful man of God. Don't think that just because a man is in a difficult place he is not a man of
God. I admire the prophet Jeremiah as much as any
man in the Bible, and he never was a success. He
prophesied at a time when Israel was in a sinful, backslidden condition, and he never was able to get her to
repent. The nation went into captivity in Egypt, and
Jeremiah was swept along with her. For 50 long years
Jeremiah faithfully preached the Word of God. His
heart was burdened for God's people! They called him
"the weeping prophet." You'd have wept too if you had
a rebellious nation on your hands, and you were unsuc-
cessfully trying to bring them back to God.

So the Lord says to this struggling pastor at
Pergamum, "That which you have already, hold fast
till I come." Hang on. Just be faithful. Then He gives
them a promise (verse 26), but we'll pass that by for
now.

Chapter 3

More Messages
From Christ
(Sardis, Philadelphia, Laodicea)

Sardis (3:1-6)

Now we come to chapter 3, verse 1, and the church at Sardis. Have you ever known churches with the names mentioned in these two chapters? Study their characteristics, and you will find out why people have so named their churches. Personally, I would never name a church Sardis, because the Lord said, "You have a name that you live, but you are dead." And yet we find some very good things about Sardis, and that is probably the reason some churches bear that name.

"Now unto the angel of the church in Sardis write: These things saith He that hath the seven Spirits of God and the seven stars." The Lord again describes Himself.

"I know thy works." Time and again He says this. He tries to commend them; He knows everything that is done for Him in any given church.

"But thou hast a name that thou livest, and art dead." You are a dead church. Many churches have a preacher and all the externals, but there is no spiritual life, no power. That church is dead, as far as God is concerned. A church may be large or small, may have much money or little, may be ornate or plain; the important thing is whether or not it has life—alive with the love and power of God.

A dear friend of mine resigned as pastor of his church. He said, "Jess, I was considered to be one of the most successful pastors. The church has a big Sunday school, with buses going out and bringing the people in. It has all the externals, but there is no spiritual power. I had to get out of it." My friend is a spiritual man. He knew that everything the church was doing could be done on the human plane. The power of God wasn't in it. It was dead. It made him sick at heart, because he is a man of God. He wanted real revival, but they were content with ritual. They did not allow the Spirit of God to use them, and he was brokenhearted about it.

Jesus said to the church at Sardis, **"Be watchful, and strengthen the things that remain that are about to die."** It was a dead church, and yet there must have been some bit of life in it, some bit of light. Jesus said they were to strengthen those things. **"For I have not found thy works perfect before God."** Do you see why God is always trying to stir us up, friends? Jesus will never let us settle down. He wants our works perfect before God. He will not let us turn in "some" fruit, when it could be "more" fruit. He is not going to let us rest until we bring forth "much" fruit, so that the Father may be glorified. He keeps stirring us up and stirring us up, individually, and collectively as a church.

"Remember, therefore, how thou hast received and heard, and hold fast, and repent." Remember, He said, what I gave you! What have we received, beloved? Everything! All that we have is a gift from God. **"What hast thou, that thou didst not receive?"** asked the Apostle Paul. Everything we have is a gift from God. **"Hold fast, and repent."** So many times He talks to the church about repentance. He is not talking to unsaved people. **"If, therefore, thou shalt not watch, I shall come on thee as a thief, and thou shalt not know what hour I will come upon thee."**

This does not refer to the second coming of Christ, as found in Revelation 19. This is His present coming in judgment. Many a time something happens to a church, and it is Christ judging that church.

"Thou hast a few names even in Sardis [our Lord knows every individual] who have not defiled their garments. [I love this next part]: And they shall walk with Me in white, for they are worthy" (v. 4). This whiteness is not the imputed righteousness of Jesus; it is our own righteous deeds. The white robes He speaks of here are our character and works as believers, not the righteousness given us by Jesus in salvation. We read at the close of this book that the fine linen garments in which we'll be dressed to meet the King are the righteous actions of the saints, the right acts and deeds of God's people. We'll be dressed according to what we have done in this life for Jesus.

I repeat, there are two kinds of righteousness. First, Christ's own righteousness that He imputes to us, puts to our account, gives to us, when we receive Him as our Savior. This is the righteousness that gets us into heaven—His righteousness. Without His righteousness we could not enter heaven. Second, there is the righteousness which is our own character and works as we live for the Lord. The Lord says, "They shall walk with Me in white, for they are worthy." And then comes the promise, which for now I will pass over.

Philadelphia (3:7-13)

Next we come to the church at Philadelphia. Jesus has nothing to rebuke in that church! It is the faithful church! From the study of church history, we may conclude that this church is found in the days of great revivals, just before the Laodicean, lukewarm days.

"To the angel [pastor] of the church at Philadelphia write: These things saith He that is holy, He that is true, He that hath the key of David, He that openeth and no man shutteth, and shutteth and no man openeth" (v. 7). The key of David means His authority, relating to God's covenant with David concerning the Kingdom. God promised the Kingdom to David. Later we will find out about how the kingdom originated, and that Jesus is the great Son of David who will bring in the Kingdom of God. So when Jesus says, "I have the key of David," it means, "I have that authority. I am the One who will fulfill God's promises to David."

Christ opens and no man shuts, shuts and no man opens. Remember that, friends, in thinking about your own life as a Christian, your opportunities and God's blessings. The Lord can open doors for you, and when He opens them nobody can shut them. Likewise, the Lord can shut doors for you, and when He shuts them nobody can open them. I often say to young people, who are thinking about God's will for their lives, that my own life has been just a series of open and shut doors. God opened doors, and I stepped through them; I did that work. Then He opened other doors, and I stepped through them and did that work. I never had to worry about it. God was leading me in His will. If He didn't open the door, I didn't try to force it and break the door down. The most frustrating thing in the world is to try to break down a door that God doesn't open. (You might find a bear in there, brother!) God's servants are immortal as long as He has given them a job to do.

Then He says, **"Thou hast a little strength."** I love that. Isn't that like Jesus to come along and say, "You have a little strength"? He doesn't quench the smoking flax. If He finds a little bit of fire, He'll try to fan it into flame. If He finds a little strength, He encourages it, and He rejoices. **"And hast kept My Word, and hast not denied My name."** Jesus commended this.

Then verse 9: **"Behold, I will make them of the synagogue of Satan [there is the adversary again, the devil, resisting Christians every inch of the way] who say they are Jews and are not, but do lie, behold, I will make them to come and worship before thy feet, and to know that I have loved thee."** Oh, how the love of Jesus comes through again! We have it more than once here.

"Because thou hast kept the word of My patience [because you have endured according to My Word], I also will keep thee from the hour of temptation [the hour of testing] which shall come upon all the world, to try [test] them that dwell upon the earth" (v. 10). That relates to the Tribulation Period. The Lord is talking about keeping them out of that time of trouble.

Not long ago I was preaching a series on Prophecy, and a preacher friend said, "Jess, where do you get the authority for the rapture of the church? I can't find it in the Bible."

Well, one great passage is Luke 12:36 where Jesus said, *"Watch and pray always that ye may be accounted worthy to escape all these things that shall come to pass, and to stand before the Son of Man."* From the context, we know He is talking about the rapture. If we are going to escape those things to come, it certainly means the rapture. "Rapture," *harpazo* in the Greek, means to be caught up, taken out of the world; because when the Tribulation strikes, it will be worldwide, with no other escape but UP. The Lord speaks clearly in that passage about escaping the Tribulation.

Then in II Thessalonians 2:7 we read, *"He that hindereth will continue to hinder until He be taken out of the way, and then shall that Wicked One be revealed."* The only thing that is holding back sin today is the Holy Spirit in the hearts of Christians, and when they are caught up to meet the Lord in the air, there will be no hindrance left on earth. Sin will spread rapidly and become worse and worse in the Tribulation. The wicked one, the Antichrist, will be revealed, and the earth will go through a period of trouble such as never before in all history. The Lord says in this verse, Revelation 3:10, "Because you have kept the word of my patience, I will keep you from the hour of testing that shall come upon all the world."

"Behold, I am coming quickly. Hold fast which thou hast, that no man take thy crown" (v. 11).

That, beloved friends, is a little "red light" to all of

us who are Christians. Someone can actually take our crown. The word "crown" relates to our works. It simply means that if we don't do the job Jesus gives us to do, He will give it to someone else, and they will get the reward. We can lose our rewards. This is beyond salvation now. The New Testament clearly distinguishes between salvation (which is by faith in Christ plus nothing) and works (which means service for Christ after we are saved). We cannot earn salvation by our works, but we are given the opportunity to serve the Lord after we have received Him as our Savior. The two—salvation and works—go together throughout the Bible. In this particular study we are not teaching what the Bible has to say about crowns; that is a long study in itself. But just let me say that the Lord speaks of five different crowns: the crown of righteousness for the godly, the crown of glory for the faithful pastor, the crown of rejoicing for the soul-winner, the incorruptible crown for the person who lives a holy life, and the crown of life for the person faithful unto death. It will bless your heart if you study these crowns for yourself in your Bible.

Laodicea (3:14-22)

Now we come to the church of Laodicea, the last of the seven churches mentioned. As we study church history and other passages of Scripture, we know that the church age will end in apostasy, a great moving away from God. We don't have time to teach it now, for it would be a whole study in itself, but Paul writes of it again and again. Peter writes of it. John writes of it. Jesus in Matthew 24:12 said, *"Because iniquity shall abound, the love of the many shall wax cold."* This passage concerning Laodicea bears out the historical interpretation that Laodicea is the church characterized by apostasy.

"Unto the angel of the church of the Laodiceans write: These things saith the Amen [that is Jesus speaking of Himself] the faithful and true witness, the beginning of the creation of God. I know thy works, that thou art neither cold nor hot. I would

that thou wert cold or hot" (v. 14,15). The Lord is saying, I wish you were one or the other, either frigid or boiling. The Lord wants us to be either absolutely for Him or against Him. He has more tolerance for somebody who says "I don't want to have anything to do with Christ" than for someone who is lukewarm, partly for Him and partly against Him. "I wish that you were either cold or hot."

"So then, because thou art lukewarm and neither cold nor hot, I will spew thee out of My mouth" (v. 16). In other words, "I cannot stomach you." He cannot have anything to do with an apostate church. This buttresses the historical teaching. All through the New Testament God warns that at the end of the church age there will be a tremendous falling away from God.

"Because thou sayest [here is what they were saying about themselves, and they were totally ignorant of their condition], I am rich and increased in goods and have need of nothing" (v. 17). They thought they had arrived. Nobody *arrives* in this world. We are not going to *arrive* until we are like Him, and we are not going to be like Him until we see Him as He is, either at death or at His return. Until then, we ought to be seeking constantly to rise higher to that perfection He tells of in the Book, "Be ye perfect, even as your Father in heaven is perfect."

"You know not that you are wretched and miserable, and poor, and blind, and naked" (v. 17). This church said, "We've got it made. We have big buildings and money and prestige in the eyes of the world." But the Lord says, "As a matter of fact, in My eyes you are wretched and miserable and poor and blind and naked."

Then He says, **"I counsel thee."** Here is Jesus giving advice to this rich church that didn't realize its poverty and shame. Three things: **"I counsel thee to buy of Me."** (This is not, of course, literal buying.) **"Buy of Me gold tried in the fire that thou mayest be rich."** He is speaking about a life of faith, for we read in Peter's epistle how faith, being tested and tried, is more precious than gold that perishes. They were also to buy from Jesus **"white raiment, that thou mayest be clothed."** That means righteousness. They were not living right. God honors those who obey His Word and live right. **"That the shame of thy nakedness do not appear. And anoint thine eyes with eyesalve that thou mayest see."** Anointing speaks of the Holy Spirit, and eyesalve means the eyes of understanding and seeing, which is the knowledge that the Holy Spirit gives when He opens our spiritual eyes.

These people needed to have a living faith in the living Christ. They needed His righteousness. They needed to live right in the eyes of God. When we are really saved people, we will pick up the Book and seek as much as possible to live according to the Word of God. One great missionary prayed, "Lord, help me to live as much a Christian life as is possible for a human being to live." God help us to live that kind of life, the Spirit-filled life, which is the result of knowing God's Word, God's mind and will, and yielding to Him.

Beloved, all the way through here our Lord calls attention to what He likes and what He dislikes. I don't know of anything more beneficial to us as Christians than to read His Word and write down the things that please Him. In this way we can check up on our lives. Let's find out what things are in our lives, attitudes and actions, that displease Him and, by His grace, get rid of them. It would reveal how much we are really pleasing the Lord. I think that is what He would have us do.

Promises to Overcomers

Now, He has made certain promises to these churches. The first promise is in Revelation 2, verse 7: **"To him that overcometh."** "Overcome" is a battle word. It means "to fight and win in battle, to conquer." The Hendley translation of "overcomer" is "winner." "To him that winneth, to the one who fights and wins in the battle of life," Jesus holds out a promise! Life is a battle. Every day you and I are fighting the world, the flesh, and the devil, and this conflict will go on until we see Jesus. If we ever sit down and say "The battle is won" this side of glory, we'll find out pretty quick that it isn't. The world, the flesh, and the devil are our three enemies every day around the clock.

What does Jesus say to the person who fights and wins, overcomes, conquers? **"I will give to eat of the tree of life, which is in the midst of the paradise of God"** (2:7). He will have a part in the Holy City. Notice the word "paradise." Paradise began with the Garden of Eden. Jesus said to the thief on the cross, "Today shalt thou be with Me in paradise." Paul said he was caught up into the third heaven, into paradise. And paradise is described in the last two chapters of the Revelation. Jesus promises that we shall be there in the Holy City if we fight and win in the battle of life through faith in Him!

The next promise, chapter 2, verse 11. **"He that overcometh shall not be hurt of the second death."** He will be exempt from the lake of fire. The person who overcomes the world, the flesh, and the devil through faith in Christ will not experience the second death.

"To him that overcometh will I give to eat of the hidden manna, and I will give him a white stone, and in the stone a new name written which no man knoweth save he that receiveth it" (v. 17). The overcomer will be given hidden manna to eat. The manna in the wilderness was a gift from God—food miraculously given to the people of Israel. There were no A&P stores out there, no drive-ins, no steak-and-shakes in the desert. Their food came from the Lord. He fed them on manna daily. "What is it?" they said, so they called it "manna," their expression for "What is it?" The Lord sustained them supernaturally.

In the Gospel of John, chapter 6, Jesus said, *"He that keeps on eating Me shall live because of Me."* The only way you and I can sustain our spiritual life is to keep the wonderful truths found in this Book about Jesus Christ in our minds, in our souls. Spiritual sustenance comes from that constant absorbing of His life into our lives, into our souls and spirits, by meditation. "He that keeps on eating Me." Have you had a meal of Jesus today? To think of that in the wrong way would be repulsive. He is not talking about cannibalism; He is talking about meditating on and taking in what Jesus has done, is doing, and will do for us. As I meditate on Him, my soul actually draws spiritual strength and sustenance from Him. The person who doesn't do that will starve to death spiritually. "He that keeps on eating Me shall live because of Me." Evidently it will be something like this in the next world. Our supernatural feeding on Christ will sustain us through the ages of eternity. The hidden manna, then, is God's miraculous sustaining of His people.

Then, **"a white stone."** I don't know what the white stone is, and I have news for you: the commentators don't either. Some of them say that in ancient times when a man's life was on trial they had a black stone and a white stone. The black stone meant condemnation; the white stone meant exoneration, that he would be freed from judgment. Other commentators refer to the gem stones in the garment of the high priest in Old Testament times. On the breastplate and shoulders were twelve stones. This is a single stone. I don't know what it is, but I know one thing—it is going to be inscribed. **"And in the stone a name written."** No one will know it except the one who receives it.

Do you have a pet name for somebody? God's pet name for Solomon was Jedidiah, which means "beloved of the Lord." God's name of endearment for Israel was Jeshurun, "My righteous one." Friends, I believe that the Lord has pet names for those who are His intimates. That name may be in the stone, for nobody will know about that name but you and Jesus. If you have someone you love, you have a pet name for him or her. It's just between the two of you. I think that may be what the Lord will have for us on that glorious day.

"He that overcometh and keepeth My works unto the end, to him will I give authority over the nations, and he shall rule them with a rod of iron.

As the vessels of a potter shall they be broken to shivers, even as I received of My Father" (2:26). That is millenarian. The Lord's gift to this overcomer is a place of rulership in the Millennium. It is mentioned also in the very last of these promises, in 3:21. **"To him that overcometh will I grant to sit with Me in My throne, even as I also overcame and have sat down with My Father in His throne."** Christ's throne is the millennial throne. Beloved, here is where we get the teaching that you and I are now, in this life, determining our place in the Millennium. I have tried to say again and again that the Lord will reward us for faithfulness. It is to the overcomer. It is to the one who fights the battle and wins.

"Him that overcometh will I make a pillar in the temple of My God, and he shall go no more out" (3:12). I love that! I love that! "He shall go no more out." Jesus said in John 14:1, "In My Father's house are many abiding places" (not mansions). There are many places to stay put, to dwell, to remain. One of these days we are going in and we'll never go out. The tragedy of Eden will never be repeated.

"And I will write upon him the name of My God, and the name of the city of My God, which is the new Jerusalem, which cometh down out of heaven from My God. And I will write upon him My new name" (v. 12). Notice that the expression "My God" is used three times here. "My God . . . My God . . . My God." I love that precious word. Oh, beloved, if we can say that God is our God, individually, how happy we should be! "MY God," our very own. David said, "O God, Thou art my God. Earnestly will I seek Thee." Daniel said, "My God has shut the lion's mouth." Paul said, "My God shall supply all your need according to His riches in glory by Christ Jesus." Thomas said, "My Lord and my God," when he saw the nail wounds in the hands of Jesus after the resurrection. Jesus said here, "I'll write upon the overcomer the name of My God." It means possession. I am the Lord's and He is mine—forever!

Cure for Lukewarmness

What is the answer to spiritual lukewarmness? Three things. First, repentance. In Revelation 3:19 Jesus says, **"As many as I love, I rebuke and chasten. Be zealous, therefore, and repent."** As we read through these statements to the seven churches, He is speaking also to us individually: **"He that hath ears to hear, let him hear."** So as I read here and find in my own life that which displeases Jesus, I must repent and get rid of it. Otherwise I will become lukewarm, and He will spew me out of His mouth. That means that fellowship is broken. I must repent. The cure for lukewarmness is confessing to Jesus and forsaking everything we are doing that displeases Him.

Second, the cure for lukewarmness is communion with Christ. Verse 20: **"Behold, I stand at the door and knock."** Literally, "I have taken My stand and remain knocking at the door." It is in the perfect tense in the Greek. He is still standing there. He doesn't walk up and knock on the door and walk away. Here is the Lord, standing outside the apostate church of Laodicea, but He is also knocking at the door of the individual heart. "Behold, I stand knocking at your heart's door." I have taken My stand and am continually knocking. **"If any man [any individual] hear My voice and open the door, I will come in to him and will dine with him, and he with Me."** Communion with the Lord! What is the answer to lukewarmness? Fellowship with Jesus! Get all sin out of the way, then renew fellowship with Him. How long has it been, beloved, since you reached out in prayer and touched Jesus Christ? Did you do it today? If there is the slightest break of fellowship, Jesus wants you to renew it. He wants to put His feet under the table and have sweet fellowship with you. When we have fellowship with Jesus, lukewarmness goes out the door.

The third cure for lukewarmness is found in verse 19. **"As many as I love, I rebuke and chasten."** If you and I are born again and in fellowship with Jesus, and then we begin to walk away, He will rebuke and chasten us. Why? Is He trying to hurt us? Oh, no. He is just trying to get us back into fellowship again. On His part, He doesn't want fellowship to be disrupted. If I continue to walk away, He will bring some worse chastening, because whom He loves He chastens, and scourges every son He receives. He loves me too much to let me get away.

Simon Peter, you remember, one time denied being a disciple of Jesus. He cursed and swore and said, "I don't even know Him." But after the resurrection Jesus came to him, and said, "Simon, do you love Me more than these?" Peter said, "Lord, You know I love You." Actually Jesus said, "Do you love Me with loyal love, Peter?"

In Greek there are two words for love, one meaning loyal love and the other meaning affectionate love. *Agapao* means "loyal love"; *phileo* means "affectionate love." Peter couldn't use the word *agapao*. He used the lower word, *phileo.* Jesus said, "Do you love Me with loyal love that will remain true?" Well, Peter remembered that at one time he had denied Him, and he said, "Lord, I love You with affectionate love." Again Jesus asked the same question, and Peter said, "Lord, You know everything. You know that I love You with this lower, affectionate love. I have affection for You, but I cannot say that I am loyal." Then Jesus came down to his level, blessed be His name, and said, "Simon Peter, do you love Me?" using the same word Peter used. And Peter said, "Lord, You know everything. You know that I love You." And Jesus said, "Well, even if you love Me with this lower love, you will prove it by feeding the lambs and the sheep." So the answer to lukewarmness is found in repentance, communion, and loving service. When fellowship is restored, we walk with the Lord Jesus Christ.

Chapter 4

The Throne Chapter

Earlier, we talked about the outline of the Book of the Revelation given in chapter 1, verse 19. *"Write the things which thou hast seen, the things which are, and the things which shall be hereafter."* The things he saw were in chapter 1. The things which "are" were the messages to the seven churches in chapters 2 and 3. The things "which shall be hereafter" are in chapters 4 through 22:5. Literally, "the things which shall be after these." It means things that will take place after the church age, which ends with the Rapture. After chapter 3, the church is not mentioned until chapter 19, where the church comes back with the Lord to the Mount of Olives. From the point of view in chapter 4, the church has already been raptured. Chapter 4 is the great throne chapter.

"After this, I looked and behold, a door was opened in heaven, and the first voice that I heard was, as it were, of a trumpet talking with me, which said, Come up here and I will show thee things which must be hereafter" (v. 1). The word translated "hereafter" is the same word we found in chapter 1, verse 19. "The things which shall be after these." Jesus said, "I am going to show you things that shall be after these things relative to the church." So the church age has ended. Prophecy is like a jigsaw puzzle. God could have put it in chronological order, but He didn't. We must put the puzzle together properly, and that is the difficulty. Someone may ask, "Why did God do that?" Well, why did He put coal deep in the earth instead of on top of the earth? In Bible study, it is good for us to have to dig to understand the Word. We would get lazy if it were all too easy for us. Prophecy is an exciting study, and especially when we see it all coming together perfectly!

So after the church is raptured, you don't see it anymore until Revelation 19:11 when the Lord Jesus comes back to this earth. After the Rapture, the next event is the Marriage Supper of the Lamb when the church is above with Christ. Then the Tribulation Period takes place on earth, the great period of trouble when the wrath of God is poured out upon an unbelieving world. It is a 7-year period, and it is called "Daniel's Seventieth Week." We'll talk more about that when we get to chapter 6.

But I want to say something more about the Rapture. It is detailed at the end of 1 Thessalonians 4: *"The Lord Himself shall descend from heaven with a shout, with the voice of the archangel, and with the trump of God: and the dead in Christ shall rise first: Then we who are alive and remain shall be caught up together with them in the clouds to meet the Lord in the air: and so shall we ever be with the Lord."* So shall we ever, ever, ever, ever, ever, ever, ever be with Jesus! I love that. And Paul added, *"Wherefore, comfort one another with these words."* It wasn't written to frighten us, but to comfort us.

One time I quoted these verses to a Christian lady and they alarmed her. Some people don't know the Gospel well enough, and they become frightened when they hear about the coming of Christ in the air. The Rapture, beloved, is our hope! It is called "the blessed hope" in the Bible. We know we are living in the last days, and it could occur at any moment. What I am trying to emphasize, however, is that the Rapture comes between chapters 3 and 4 of the Revelation.

Now let's outline the next four chapters. Chapter 4 is the throne chapter. In chapter 5, Christ the Lamb in the midst of the throne takes a book out of the right hand of the Father. It is the book of the end. He begins to tear away the seven seals. Chapter 6 tells of six seal judgments. The seal judgments are the first of three great judgments: the seal judgments, the trumpet judgments, and the bowl judgments. At the tearing off of the seventh seal, the six trumpet judgments begin. After the seventh trumpet come the seven bowl judgments, which will bring to an end the wrath of God that will be poured out upon an unbelieving world.

So chapter 4 is the great *throne* chapter. I love to read this over and over. One man of God said that every Sunday morning when he got up, before he had breakfast, he would read this 4th chapter of Revelation. He said, "I want to remind myself before I go to preach that God is sovereign! He is sitting on His throne, and I am to preach His Word. When I am preaching His Word, He is backing me up."

There are four major *throne* chapters in the Bible: Isaiah 6, where Isaiah saw the Lord, high and lifted up, upon His throne; Ezekiel 1, where Ezekiel saw visions of God; Daniel 7, where Daniel saw God give the world to His Son; and Revelation 4, which we have here. Verse 1: **"Behold, a door was opened in heaven."** It is wonderful to study "doors" mentioned in Scripture. Here is a door of heaven! John hears the voice of Jesus, the same voice that spoke to him in chapter 1.

"And the first voice which I heard was, as it were, of a trumpet talking with me, saying, Come up here, and I will show you things which must be after these things." [things Jesus wanted John to write] (v. 1). This heaven is the third heaven. There are three heavens: the heaven of the atmosphere around us, the heaven of space and the stars, and the third heaven which is the dwelling place of God.

John was immediately ushered into the presence of God. John was in the Spirit when this occurred (4:2). Perhaps this was an experience similar to that of the apostle Paul who said in II Corinthians 14, *"I was caught up into the third heaven and heard things unlawful for a man to utter."* So we know of two men down here on earth, Paul and John, who were caught up into the third heaven while they were still alive, and they came back down and continued in the ministry God had assigned to them.

John said, **"I was in the Spirit."** Literally, "I became in Spirit." That was his way of saying that the Spirit of God absolutely controlled him. There are various human theories about the inspiration of the Bible. But don't give me the reasonings of men about divine inspiration. I will take exactly what God says, and God says here that John was under the absolute control of the Spirit of God. John was under His control, too, when he wrote these words. That's enough for me. The Spirit of God within my heart bears witness that this is the Word of the living God. Your theory of inspiration depends on the state of your heart before God. Whenever I find anybody casting a shadow over the person of the Lord Jesus Christ or over the Word of God, they are not for me. I don't belong to that crowd.

"I was in the Spirit, and behold, a throne" (v. 2). Here was John, banished to the Isle of Patmos by the Emperor Domitian, who said, if tradition is correct, "I'll put that man John out of business. I'll send him over there on the island to work in the mines." And on a certain Sunday, the Lord took John out of himself. I don't know if, like Paul, he was in the body or out of the body, but he was definitely in the Spirit, and the Spirit of God controlled him and took him literally up into the third heaven, into the very presence of God. And what did he see? He saw God sitting upon His throne! Brother, if God were to say to me, "Jess, 5 minutes from now I am going to let you have that experience," I'd say, "Goodby, folks! See you later!" One of these days, beloved, I am going to go there. And you will too by the grace of God. Oh, how wonderful it is to know that, for we have the promise from Jesus.

John saw the very throne of God. Think of the majesty of the throne of God! God has given this to us in His Word so that we may not be afraid but have the fearless heart that Jesus so often mentioned. He was constantly telling His people, "Fear not. Don't be afraid. Let not your heart be troubled." Friends, many of us are troubled because we have *not* seen God sitting on the throne in absolute authority over this universe. I want to tell you that not even the devil himself nor all demons nor all wicked men can ever push God off His throne! He is "the Throne Sitter."

The first time I read this, my heart quickened. John saw GOD? I said, "Here I'm going to learn what God looks like!" What *does* God look like? When John gazed on that throne, all he saw was a blaze of light and color coming from that throne.

"And He that sat was to look upon like a jasper [diamond, crystal-white], and a sardine stone [carnelian red]; and there was a rainbow round about the throne, in sight like unto an emerald" (v.3). White and red and green were all flashing forth from the throne of God. That is as far as John went. Is that a perfect description of God? Oh, no, no! God let John see only the blaze of glory shining from the throne. I repeat, beloved friends, that the devil and demons and wicked men will never keep God from doing whatever He wants to do. God is sovereign! And *out* of Him, and *through* Him, and *unto* Him, are all things. He is OUR God, and He will BE God forever! What a comfort to our hearts!

John then speaks about the twenty-four elders around the throne. I call them "Presbyterians," because the Greek word is *presbuteros.* It means "old man." **"Around the throne were twenty-four thrones [seats] and upon the thrones [seats] I saw twenty-four elders sitting, clothed in white raiment and on their heads crowns of gold"** (v. 4). White raiment symbolizes absolute purity. Some of our dear brethren say that the color of heaven is blue; I say that the color of heaven is white, all the way through the Book. These twenty-four presbyters were in white raiment and had on their heads crowns of gold. One reason we believe that these were human beings is that the word translated "crown" here does not mean "diadem." There are two words for "crown" in Greek. One is *diadema,* which has to do with sovereignty and absolute power. The other is *stephanos,* the kind of crown given to a victor in the games. In the ancient Greek games they would place a wreath of leaves upon the head of the man who won the contest, the race, the wrestling match, or whatever. Those leaves would fade. Paul alludes to this in referring to athletics. There are some ten or fifteen Greek words about athletics, and one of these has to do with this word *stephanos,* the victor's crown. Paul said in I Corinthians 9:25, *"They do it to obtain a corruptible crown,"* the garland of leaves that soon fades and withers. *"But we, an incorruptible crown,"* one that doesn't fade away. The crown that God will give us for overcoming will never pass away. So this is the victor's crown, and the victor had to do some fighting to obtain it. These twenty-four elders, therefore, were victors in their earthly life, and here they are sitting on twenty-four seats around the throne.

There is a difference of opinion about who they are. Most expositors believe they are representatives of the church, raptured and enthroned in heaven. That is the usual interpretation, and it is supported by the use of the word "crown" here, *stephanos,* which was given to victors, ones who overcame the world, the flesh, and the devil.

"And out of the throne proceeded lightnings and thunderings and voices: and there were seven lamps of fire (translate the word "lamps" here, "torches") burning before the throne, which are the seven Spirits of God" (v. 5). At least three times in the Bible the Holy Spirit is spoken of as seven Spirits. This seems strange to us. But don't make any fixed rules and limits about Bible study, friends. Take just exactly what God says. There is only one Holy Spirit, the third member of the Godhead—God the Father, God the Son, and God the Holy Spirit. The Holy Spirit is co-equal with the Father and the Son. He is God. He is a person. He is not just an influence. He is not an "it." He is not a feeling. He is a person, because He loves. Attributes of personality are given to Him which can be given to none but a real person. The Holy Spirit is a person, and this refers to His sevenfold operation. In Isaiah 11:2 we read these words about Christ: *"And the spirit of the Lord shall rest upon Him, the spirit of wisdom and understanding, the spirit of counsel and might, the spirit of knowledge and of the fear of the Lord."* Evidently this is the Holy Spirit in His sevenfold operation. He rests upon Christ, gives wisdom, understanding, counsel, strength, knowledge, and the fear of (reverence for) the Lord.

"And before the throne there was a sea of glass like unto crystal: and in the midst of the throne, and round about the throne were four beasts" (v. 6). The word translated "beast" suggests an animal, but these are not animals. They are four super-earthly beings. In God's order, there are various kinds of beings, other than human beings. There are angels, such as Michael the archangel, and Gabriel the special messenger who stands before God. As we go through this, we'll find some wonderful teachings about angels. In Isaiah 6 we read about the cherubim and the seraphim in Isaiah's vision of God high and lifted up in the temple. These are super-earthly beings. Now these four beings, called beasts, are in the Greek four *zoa*, from the Greek word meaning "life." There are two words for life: *bios,* from which we get our word "biology." Biology is the study of animal and plant life around us. The other word is *zoe,* from which we get our word zoology, the study of animal life. This is the word used here. It is the more intimate word and one that relates to eternal life. So these are four living super-beings—not animals.

These four beings round about the throne were **"full of eyes, before and behind. The first was like a lion [suggesting power], the second like a calf [suggesting service], the third had a face like a man [suggesting intelligence], and the fourth was like a flying eagle [suggesting sovereignty, for an eagle soars above all]."** We find a similar description in Ezekiel, chapter 1.

Each of these four living creatures had **"six wings about him; and they were full of eyes within: and they rest not day nor night,"** but are ceaselessly active. No one has to sleep in heaven. They keep **"saying, Holy, holy, holy, Lord God Almighty, which was, and is, and is to come."** The hymn that we sing, "Holy, Holy, Holy," comes from this verse. Notice that the word "holy" is said three times. What does holy mean? What do you mean by a holy person? Holy means without sin. God is perfectly holy. He never thinks wrong, speaks wrong, or does wrong. He never has, and He never will. He is the thrice-holy God. One of Isaiah's favorite terms for God is "The Holy One of Israel." How amazing, then, that God comes along and calls us "saints," when the word "saint" means "holy"! It's because of Jesus! We are not holy in ourselves. But He is holy in Himself. Nobody on this earth is holy in himself or herself. We can be holy only by receiving Christ's righteousness by faith. Then God calls us saints.

When I came in tonight, I saw a dear lady who was a member of our church years ago. I said, "My, it is good to see you, Saint _____ ," calling her by name. She said, "No, no." But I said, "Yes, you are a saint, for God says so." We look at ourselves and see our faults and failures and we say we are not saints because we think that term means perfection. We are not perfect. But, as believers in Christ, we have been given the perfection of Christ, and He sees us as He sees Him! Hebrews 10:14 says, **"For by one offering [on the cross], He hath perfected forever them that are [being] sanctified."** Perfected forever! So I dare say that I am

Saint Jess, and you can say, if you are a believer, that you are Saint _____ , whatever your name is. But the only way we can say that is by believing God's Word. If God didn't say it, I wouldn't say it. Remember, that doesn't mean we are perfect. We are not. But we are in Christ, and when God looks at me He sees Jesus, and Jesus looks good to Him. I don't look very good, but Jesus certainly does!

"Holy, holy, holy, Lord God Almighty." YAHWEH, Elohim, Sabaoth, in the Hebrew. The word "Almighty" here is the same word we found previously in relation to Christ, meaning "the One who holds all things in His grasp." These four living creatures say, "Holy, holy, holy, Lord God Almighty" to the One sitting on the throne who holds all things in His grasp, the God of the universe. Now, this is focusing on God the Father. This One on the throne is not Christ. This is not the Spirit. The attention is upon God the Father on the throne, and He is the Lord God Almighty. Can you imagine His power, holding everything in His grasp? Beloved, if HE is on our side, who can be against us? "What have I to dread, what have I to fear/ Leaning on the everlasting arms?/ I have blessed peace with my Lord so near;/ Leaning on the everlasting arms." It is said of Jacob (Genesis 49) that the arms of his hands were made strong by the mighty hands of the God of Jacob. These poor hands couldn't hold up anything; but underneath them, unseen, are the strong arms of God! Oh, the throne! The throne!

Verse 9: Those living creatures **"give glory and honor and thanks to Him that sat on the throne, who liveth forever and ever."** Literally, "Who liveth unto the ages of the ages." Here is the very strongest Greek phrase for "unendingness." The Greek speaks of an age (singular) as a long period of time. Ages (plural) are long periods of time after long periods of time. Here he speaks of "unto the ages of the ages," which is the strongest phrase in any language for *unendingness.* Beloved, wouldn't it be a tragedy if all of this wonder and all of this revelation about God and His glorious salvation revealed in His Word were to last for only a century, or for only a millennium? As long as God lives (and that is forever and ever), His salvation will abide! And when you and I, poor sinners as we are, come to Him believing His Word, repenting of our sins and receiving Christ as our Savior and Lord, that very moment God gives us THE GIFT—you know what it is—ETERNAL LIFE! How long does eternal life last? As long as God Himself lives!

God gave me the gift of eternal life 48 years ago one day when I was sitting on the porch of a little house near Atlanta. That day He opened my eyes, He opened my heart, and I received Jesus. That day God gave me the gift of His own life, and because I have His life, I shall live unto the ages of the ages! If God dies, I am in trouble. But God isn't going to die—ever.

"The four and twenty elders fall down before Him that sat on the throne, and worship Him that liveth forever and ever, and cast their crowns before the throne, saying, "Thou art worthy, O Lord" (v. 10). The word "worthy" in its root meaning means "valuable." And who is the Most Valuable Being in this universe? God! And what is the most valuable thing to us in this universe? Eternal life! Yet little worldlings run around sacrificing the eternal for the present. They sacrifice eternal life for liquor and dope and lust and a thousand other things that are simply like husks that swine eat, and they reject this wonderful God and His great salvation. They are like a character in John Bunyan's *Pilgrim's Progress*—the man with the muckrake. You know what muck is; it's mud and dirt and filth. This man spends all his time raking in the muck and mud and dirt, when all the while over his head is a beautiful angel offering him real life. The man never sees him, because he never looks up. There are worlds of people like that. In spite of all that God and Christ and the Holy Spirit and God's servants can do, they just will not look up! They are going to keep on raking muck, right on into hell.

Let me call your attention to the word "worship." So

often this word is misused. I am talking about people who go to a church where the music or other atmosphere stirs the emotions, and they leave the service saying, "My, we worshiped today." A church can have all those things and never worship God. To worship is to adore God. It is the prostration of the spirit in adoration of God. If our hearts have not reached out to HIM in humility and praise for all that He has done for us in giving us life in this present world and eternal life in Jesus, we have not worshiped. The Greek word for "worship" means "to bow the knees."

These twenty-four elders worshiped, bowed the knees, before Him that liveth forever and ever, and they cast their crowns before the throne, saying: **"Thou art worthy, O Lord, to receive glory, and honor, and power: for Thou hast created all things, and for Thy pleasure they are [they exist] and were created"** (v. 11). They praise God, these beings in heaven, for the gift of life, existence. How many people ever thank God just for life? A lot of people fuss at God and pout with God and get mad at God. But how many thank Him for the gift of life? "Lord, You created us for Your pleasure." Why am I made? Not for my pleasure. Somebody said, "I am made for myself, so I will draw a circle around myself and I'll just do anything I want to do." Well, that is selfishness, and it ends in corruption and finally in hell if it is persisted in. We are made, beloved, for God's pleasure. And the wonderful thing about it is that in pleasing Him we find our true pleasure. No other place can it be found but in Him. Who is to be Number One in our lives? God—He that sitteth upon the throne!

Chapter 5

Christ, the Lamb

The Book of the End

In chapter 5 we have Christ the Lamb in the midst of the throne. From here on, it is constantly God and the Lamb, God and the Lamb. The kingdom belongs to God and the Lamb, all the way to the close of the book. God and the Lamb and the Spirit, all three are found in the last chapter of the Revelation.

"And I saw in the right hand of Him that sat on the throne a book [scroll] written within and on the backside, sealed with seven seals" (v. 1). There are several references to books in the New Testament, and we must discern what they are. This book in the hand of God is the Book of the End, the book of successive events. We will be studying about these tremendous events that move through the Tribulation Period, to the second coming of Christ, the final revolt of Satan, the great white throne judgment, the destruction of the heavens and the earth, the creation of the new heavens and earth, and the Holy City coming down from God out of heaven. It is all written in this "book."

This is not a book in the modern sense. It is a roll, or scroll. In those days they didn't have books like ours today. They had parchment. They would roll it as they were writing on it; and when reading, they would unroll it. It has been estimated that this roll must have been some fifteen feet in length. What a precious roll it was, sealed with seven seals on the outside. We will find out about its contents as we go along. This scroll is in the right hand of God the Father, who is sitting on the throne. It has seven seals. You seal up something when you don't want anybody to tamper with it. When you write a love letter to your sweetheart, you seal it. By that you mean that nobody else should open it. A sealed article is only for the one for whom it is intended. Seals mean privacy, not to be opened.

So we read in verse 2, **"And I saw a strong angel"** (Here is another angel; we will find much angelic activity in this book) **"proclaiming with a loud voice, Who is worthy to open the book, and to loose the seals thereof?"** With a loud voice! I have a message called "Heaven Is a Noisy Place." It came from a study of this Book of the Revelation. The angel said, "Who is worthy to open the book and loose the seals?" Who is worthy to step up and take the book of the end, the book of the consummation, out of the Father's hand and begin to tear open the seals and supervise the tremendous judgments of the endtime that God must bring to pass before He can bring us world peace?

Who is worthy? I'm not. Do you think I'm going to step up there and take that book and start tearing off the seals that bring the judgments of God on this earth? In one judgment alone, one billion people will die! Do you think I am worthy to pass judgment on a billion people? I am not worthy to pass judgment on anybody! Who is worthy to judge this world? Only a sinless person is worthy to judge sinners. We are so inconsistent. We have a proverb that says, "People who live in glass houses should not throw stones." That's right. Jesus said to a crowd of wicked men one time, "Let him that is without sin among you cast the first stone." They were judging a sinner when they themselves were sinners, and they began to slink out of His presence, leaving the accused woman at His feet. We are all sinners, and we have no right to judge each other. God condemns censorious judgment. *"Judge not, that ye be not judged. For with what judgment ye judge, ye shall be judged. With what measure ye mete, it shall be measured to you again"* (Matthew 7:1,2). Jesus alone is the judge. God says that all judgment has been committed into the hands of His Son. God is going to judge the world through Jesus. The Man of the Cross will be the Judge of the World.

Verse 3: **"And no man in heaven, nor in earth, neither under the earth [hell] was found able to open the book, neither to look thereon."** Notice the three divisions: heaven, earth, and under the earth. "Under the earth" means hell, which is in the heart of the earth. Nobody was found worthy, because everybody but Jesus is a sinner. God charges His angels with folly, and even the stars are not pure in His sight. He is an absolutely holy being. What we need today is more preaching about the holiness of God! We hear so much about the love of God, and it needs to be balanced with the holiness of God.

Notice the tears of John. I love this about him. **"I wept [profusely] because no man was found worthy to open and to read the book, neither to look thereon. And one of the elders saith unto me, Weep not [literally, Stop crying, John] behold, the Lion of the tribe of Juda, the Root of David, hath prevailed to open the book and to loose the seven seals thereof."**

Jesus the Lamb

Verse 6: **"And I beheld, and, lo, in the midst of the throne and of the four [living creatures], and in the midst of the elders, stood a Lamb."** In verse 5 Jesus is called a Lion. In verse 6 He is called a Lamb. How can this be? Some people become confused in reading the Bible or in their thinking about God and Christ, because they fail to take into account these two truths, that in God and in Christ are two characteristics: lionlike and lamblike.

Let me illustrate. A blind person is about to cross a street. A policeman stops traffic and leads this blind person gently and safely to the other side. A few moments later there is a holdup down the street. A man with a gun is shooting people. The policeman now must pull out his gun and kill him to keep him from killing other people. When he leads the blind person across the street, that is his lamblike character; when he shoots a person who is killing others, that is his lionlike character. Both are righteous acts. Jesus is the Lion of Judah as well as the Lamb of God. Don't forget it—God is a God of holiness as well as a God of love, and these two never violate each other. God is just and righteous in both. They go together. There is no other way you can interpret your Bible. When God drowned the world in Noah's day and spared only eight people, that was His lionlike character. But He did it in love to spare unborn generations from corruption. God never judges until He must. And when He hits, He hits hard.

Jesus is like that, we learn from the Gospels. Some people, because they don't know Him and don't know the Bible, have a misconception about Jesus. They think that He always said the sweet, kind word. I want to tell you something, friend. There wasn't a smile on Jesus' face when He wrapped the leather thongs around His hand and drove those money-changers out of the temple and said, *"Take these things out of here! My house shall be called the house of prayer, but ye have made it a den of thieves!"* And I want to tell you, there wasn't a smile on His face when He said to the scribes, *"Woe unto you scribes, Pharisees, hypocrites!"* I defy you to find in literature such scathing, blistering, burning words as you find in Matthew 23, as He lashes out against the hypocrisy of the religious leaders of His day! Our Lord didn't always say the gentle, kind things, and someday He is going to judge this world with severe judgment! Because of His love, He died for sinners; but because of His righteousness, He must judge and clean up this world. Jesus is both Lamb and Lion!

He is also called, here in verse 5, the Root of David, in connection with the Davidic Covenant. We must understand the great covenants of God with men, to understand the Bible. The covenant with Abraham concerns the land of Israel and the people. The covenant with David concerns the perpetual kingdom. The Palestinian covenant concerns the giving of the land to the people of Israel, which belongs to them in perpetuity. Then the covenant that we have, praise God, *"This is My blood of the New Covenant,"* is in Matthew 27. There's not a more precious study in the Bible than that of the covenants.

Jesus here is called the Root of David. Not David himself, but David's greater Son, Jesus, will inherit this world. David will have a part, as we're going to see. But Jesus is the Lamb who will be King—Jesus, the Son of God, the One who submitted to being spat upon and beaten and mistreated and dragged away to a cruel cross to die.

This is Jesus, the Lamb **"as it had been slain"** (v. 6). That phrase means "as it had been freshly slaughtered." It is in the perfect tense, an action in the past that still continues in effect. It means that He carries the evidence of His crucifixion into glory. This is my own thinking, but I have reason to believe it is true: in the new world, where all sin will be blotted out and wherein nothing will dwell but righteousness, the only evidence of sin will be the marks of our Lord's crucifixion. We will see the thorn-wounds in His brow, the spear-wound in His side, the nail-wounds in His hands and feet. Fanny Crosby wrote, "I shall know Him, I shall know Him, as redeemed by His side I shall stand; I shall know Him, I shall know Him, by the print of the nails in His hands."

I don't wish to offend our friends who are Roman Catholics, but there was a little lady who was worried about her sins and she went to a priest. He said, "Come into the confessional and confess your sins to me, and I will forgive you of your sins." She drew back indignantly and said, "Sir! The only One who can forgive me of

my sins has nail wounds in His hands!'' Yes! The dear
One with the nail wounds in His hands is the only One
who can forgive me of my sins. Blessed be His name!

Verse 6: There stood a Lamb, as it had been
slaughtered, **"having seven horns."** That is His
power. Horn suggests power in the Hebrew. **"And
seven eyes."** That is His intelligence. **"Which are the
seven Spirits of God sent forth into all the earth."**
Aren't you glad He sent the Holy Spirit to the earth to
call out a people for His name, the church of the Lord
Jesus? I want to say to my fellow preachers, when you
and I stand up to preach and try to present Christ to
this lost world, we have enemies—the world, the flesh
and the devil. But we also have God on our side. We
have the Word of God and Christ and the Holy Spirit.
Jesus is with us and in our midst.

The Lamb Takes the Book

**"And He [the Lamb] came and took the book out
of the right hand of Him that sat upon the throne"**
(v. 7). This is Jesus coming up to the Father and taking
the book of the end. Jesus Christ our Lord will supervise
the events of the consummation, all the way through to
the new heaven and the new earth! Don't miss Jesus as
you read the Revelation, for He is the center of all the
drama.

Verse 8: **"And when He had taken the book, the
four beasts [living creatures] and four and twenty
elders fell down before the Lamb."** That is worship:
prostration before Jesus. If our hearts have not gone
out in prostration to God and Jesus in abject worship as
unworthy sinners, in love and adoration that He saved
us, we have not worshiped. The elders fell down before
the Lamb, **"having every one of them harps [lyres,
stringed instruments], and golden [bowls] full of
[perfume], which are the prayers of saints."** The
subject of prayer is coming later, but what a precious
thing to know that our prayers are a perfume in God's
nostrils! When a lady comes through the room, and she
has just come from cosmetizing, you are aware of a

sweet fragrance as she passes by. That's what happens, beloved, when we pray. Our prayers are a sweet fragrance to God.

Jesus Worthy

Verse 9: **"And they sang a new song, saying, Thou art worthy."** Thou art valuable. Verse 11 of the preceding chapter says that God the Father sitting on the throne is the Most Valuable Person. Here Christ the Lamb is given equal value, which emphasizes His deity! Our blessed Jesus was indeed a man, but don't you forget it, friend, HE IS GOD, co-equal with the Father. **"Thou art worthy to take the book, and to open the seals thereof: for Thou wast slain, and hast redeemed us to God."** You were killed and You bought us to God. That is what the word "redeemed" means; *agorazo*, "to buy out of the marketplace." He paid the price of His blood to set us free from sin, death, judgment, and hell. We are free! Blessed be God! Let's hold up our heads and throw out our chests, for we are somebody! Jesus made us somebody. He doesn't expect us to go crawling around like bugs on the ground. He elevated us and gave us significance.

"Thou wast slain and hast bought us to God." Our King James Version is not taken from the earliest and best Greek readings, so some small changes, but very important ones, need to be made. The word "us" ought not to be here in the text, because these living creatures are not saying, "You have bought us," but **"You bought to God, by Your blood, people out of every kindred and tongue and people and nation."** You bought to God people from all over this world, of every culture, every color, and every race, **"and hast made them unto our God kings and priests; and we shall reign on the earth."** The redeemed shall reign on the earth! I don't know whether you believe that or not. We consider ourselves nonentities, and in ourselves that is what we are. But we shall reign because Jesus redeemed us. Do you know what "reign" means? It means to rule, to be in authority. Do you believe you are going to be a king? Well, God says you are! Christ made

us kings and priests unto God and His Father. We shall reign as kings forever and ever.

Beloved, this is so wonderful that it's hard to comprehend unless we meditate on it and meditate on it and pray over it till we actually believe it. Faith comes by hearing, and hearing by the Word of God. And the more we study the Word of God, the more faith increases, till finally we actually believe that we poor sinners who deserve hell have been redeemed and so elevated by the Lord Jesus that God says we are going to reign as kings forever and ever!

Verse 11: **"And I beheld, and I heard the voice of many angels round about the throne and the [living creatures] and elders: and the number was ten thousand times ten thousand, and thousands of thousands."** The Greek says "myriads of myriads, and thousands of thousands beyond myriads," which means unnumbered, incalculable, millions of these heavenly beings.

"Saying with a loud voice, Worthy is the Lamb that was slain to receive power, and riches, and wisdom, and strength, and honor, and glory, and blessing. And every creature that is in heaven, and on earth, and under the earth [in hell], and such as are in the sea, and all that are in them, heard I saying, Blessing, and honor, and glory, and power, be unto Him that sitteth upon the throne [God the Father], and unto the Lamb [the Lord Jesus Christ] forever and ever [unto the ages of the ages]." That is a fulfillment of Paul's word in the Philippian letter chapter 2, that "every knee shall bow and every tongue confess that Jesus Christ is Lord, to the glory of God the Father."

So in chapter 4, John saw God. Here in chapter 5, he saw Christ take out of the hands of the Father, the Book of the End and begin to tear off those seals, supervising the consummation. Who has the book in His hands now? Who is worthy? The One who died on the cross to save sinners! HE is the only One worthy and able to judge sinners aright.

Chapter 6

The Meaning of the Seals

Six Seals

We come now to chapter 6, and we have Jesus beginning to tear the seals. **"And I saw when the Lamb
opened one of the seals, and I heard, as it were the
noise of thunder, and one of the four [living
creatures] saying, Come. . . . And I saw, and behold
a white horse: and he that sat on it had a bow; and a
crown was given unto him: and he went forth
conquering, and to conquer."** This is not Christ, because He cannot be the One supervising from heaven
during the time of the end and also be the one coming at
the same time. He does come on a white horse in chapter 19, verse 11. Till then, He is in heaven supervising
the events of the endtime.

This rider on the white horse is the Antichrist, the
man of sin. (We'll not give you the Scriptures on that
now because we are coming to a great passage about
him in Revelation 13.) The rider here is the Antichrist
upon a white horse, suggestive of his military power,
and wearing a crown, symbolizing that he will rule this
world the last three and a half years of the Tribulation
before Jesus comes back to earth. *"And he went forth*

conquering." He is going to conquer this world! Nobody will be able to make war with the beast. *"And to conquer,"* but he will be brought to his end by Jesus. You have heard of the Four Horsemen of the Apocalypse? (Apocalypse means Revelation.) Here is the first of the four.

Second Seal

Verse 3: **"And when he had opened the second seal, I heard the second [living creature] say, Come. . . . And there went out another horse that was red [blood red, the Greek says]: and power was given him that sat thereon to take peace from the earth, and that they should kill one another: and there was given unto him a great sword."** Do you know what that says, friends? It describes a world that is in total violence. Peace will be taken from the earth. In our presidential election years we hear a lot about peace. The leaders say, "Put me into office and I'll bring peace." We will not have peace. God's Word says that instead of things getting better they are going to get worse, and that as soon as the church is caught up to meet the Lord in the air the Tribulation Period will come. There will be no peace on the earth. Violence will cover this earth. I shudder to think about it. Thank God, the church will be up there with Jesus when all this breaks forth on the earth.

Third Seal

Now the third seal, verse 5. **"And when He had opened the third seal, I heard the third [living creature] say, Come. . . . And I beheld, and lo a black horse: and he that sat on him had a pair of balances in his hand. And I heard a voice in the midst of the four [living creatures] say, A measure of wheat for a penny, and three measures of barley for a penny; and see that thou hurt not the oil and the wine."** Famine! Antichrist is coming and he'll ride on the white horse; he's the false Christ. He'll ride on the blood-red horse, war and violence over all the earth. Then the black horse, famine stalking the earth, food so scarce that it will have to be measured out. A penny, or denarius, was the daily wage of a laborer in John's day. If the average family has four, what will happen to the other three if a man can buy only enough for himself? What will happen to his wife and children? The famine will be worldwide. We here in America hardly know what famine means. When I was in India I saw some sights so pitiful that I won't describe them to you. If I were a young Christian today, do you know what I would do if my wife would go with me? We'd go to India. I could give my life to those pitiful people. Famine!

Fourth Seal

"And when He had opened the fourth seal, I heard the voice of the fourth [living creature] saying, Come. . . . And I looked, and behold a pale horse [pale green, the picture of death]: and his name that sat on him was Death, and Hades [hell] followed with him. And power was given unto them over the fourth part of the earth, to kill with sword, and with hunger, and with death, and with the beasts of the earth" (vv. 7,8).

They tell us that there are more than four billion people on this planet today. The latest census is four and one-half billion, and increasing. But let's say four billion. One-fourth of four billion is one billion. If the projected population increase is correct, there will be six billion people on this earth by the year 2,000—if Jesus tarries until that time. In chapter 9, another third of the rest of the earth is destroyed. That tallies up to one-half of the population of this world who will die in the Great Tribulation Period within three and a half years before Jesus returns. We are going to find out why God permits this. A fourth of the earth, one billion souls, will die in this one judgment and go to hell. It says that hell follows in its train.

Now, that prophecy ought to do two things. First, if you are unsaved, it ought to bring you to Christ! Second, if we are saved, it ought to make us love souls and try to win as many others as we can to Jesus.

Fifth Seal

Verse 9: **"And when He had opened the fifth seal, I saw under the altar."** This altar was in the heavenly sanctuary. When Moses was up in the mountain with God, God gave him the plan for the tabernacle, which the people of Israel were to carry with them through the wilderness. It was also the plan for the temple to come. God said, "Be sure to make it like the pattern that I showed you in the mountain. Make it after the pattern of the heavenly temple." We are going to read more about this heavenly sanctuary, but here is the altar that John saw. Under the altar were **"the souls of them that were slain [people martyred during the Tribulation] for the word of God, and for the testimony which they held."** So during the Tribulation the Word of God will be preached. There will be the testimony of the Word of God. And the testimony of Christ will be given. These people will die for standing for God and Christ and the Word during the Tribulation. These are not church saints, for they are in heaven; these are Tribulation saints.

Verse 10: **"And they cried with a loud voice, saying, How long, O Lord, holy and true, dost Thou not judge and avenge our blood on them that dwell on the earth?"** You say, "Could they be Christians? Do souls of people in heaven cry out to God for vengeance on others?" Friends, we must revise our ideas about God, if we have preconceived notions without examining the truths in God's Word. The great Bible teacher Dr. G. Campbell Morgan said (and my experience has borne witness to it), "The older I get, when I take a text of Scripture I have to have the whole Bible to back it up." In other words, you cannot just take a text of Scripture and interpret it alone.

Let me give you an illustration. You may have heard it before, but let me repeat it. The Bible says that Judas went out and hanged himself. It also says (in another place), "Go thou and do likewise." And in another place, "What thou doest, do quickly." Now, all three of those are indeed Scriptures. But if you accept them in that order you will go out and hang yourself and be in a hurry to do it! Silly as it is, it shows how some people take the Bible and make it mean anything. We are to rightly divide the Word of God, not distort it and twist it, not take things out of their context. We are to study the whole counsel of God and bring it together in its proper order. If we do, it will fit perfectly, like a jigsaw puzzle. It always does.

Now, God doesn't rebuke these martyred souls when they cry out, "How long, O Lord, before You avenge our blood upon those murderers down there, who hate You and Your Christ and Your Word and Christians and Christian testimony?" In this church age, God tells us, *"Love your enemies, bless them that curse you, do good to them that hate you, and pray for them that despitefully use you, and persecute you"* (Matthew 5:44). But they are allowed to do in heaven what we are not allowed to do now. We must know to whom the Lord is speaking. We must know the dispensation, the time period. We must put the proper thing in the proper pigeonhole, or we get into trouble. These people were righteous in what they were saying in heaven.

Verse 11: **"And white robes were given unto every one of them."** Now, it is said that these are souls under the altar. So, obviously their bodies were killed and were either buried or went back to the dust on earth. Nothing but their souls are there. Will you tell me how you can robe a soul? Robes were given unto them. Can you put a robe around a spirit, a soul, an intangible being? We are body, soul, and spirit. Soul and spirit are intangible. I am a soul and spirit, speaking through this body. The body is just a vehicle of expression. I am looking out of these eyes and speaking through this mouth and hearing through these ears and moving through these hands and feet. But my body is not me. I am more than body. When my body dies, I am still going to be a spirit and soul, living forever! So are you.

Scholars have been conferring for a long time whether the Bible teaches that there may be an intermediate, temporary body when we die. I never will forget the first time I read through my Greek Testament and came to II Corinthians 5:1, which says, *"If our earthly house of this tabernacle were dissolved, we have a building of God, an house not made with hands, eternal in the heavens."* The thing that gave me trouble was the Greek word *echomen,* "we have." It is present tense. It may mean that the minute this tabernacle (body) is dissolved, we have a house not made with hands, eternal in the heavens. I began to reason about it myself, and I was glad to discover that some scholars believe there is a temporary body, before the everlasting body which will be given to us at the resurrection. On the Mount of Transfiguration, Moses and Elijah appeared to Peter, James, and John, with the Lord Jesus in the midst. Were Moses and Elijah just spirits? Or did they have a temporary body?

These souls under the altar were given white robes. Verse 11: **"And it was said unto them that they should rest yet for a little season, until their fellowservants also and their brethren, that should be killed as they were, should be fulfilled."** They said, "Lord, when are You going to avenge us?" and the Lord answered, "Just rest awhile. There will be more martyrs just like you, and when the proper time comes, I will deal justly with that crowd that murdered them and you."

Did you know that there is such a thing in the Bible as holy vengeance? I preached on that one time, and a godly lady took me to task about it. She said, "I don't believe that God and Jesus would take vengeance." I told her very kindly, "It's in the Book." She still didn't believe me. Some people have such preconceived notions that even when you show them the Scripture they won't believe it. *"Vengeance is Mine. I will repay, saith the Lord"* (Romans 12:19). And He is going to do it one of these days.

Sixth Seal

"And I beheld when He had opened the sixth seal, and, lo, there was a great earthquake; and the

sun became black as sackcloth of hair, and the
moon became as blood; and the stars of heaven fell
unto the earth, even as a fig tree casteth her un-
timely figs when she is shaken of a mighty wind.
And the heaven departed as a scroll when it is
rolled together; and every mountain and island
were moved out of their places" (vv. 12-14).

One of the greatest catastrophes that this world has
ever known was when the Island of Krakatau near
Java suddenly disappeared in a terrific explosion.
Large areas were inundated, killing people right and
left. Tidal waves 150 feet high lashed the shore and
were driven out all over the world. They were felt even
in South America and Hawaii. More people died in that
catastrophe than in most any other that has happened
on this earth.

Verse 14 here says that *every* island and mountain
was moved out of its place! A terrific judgment! The
sun is blackened, the light goes out, the moon becomes
like blood, the stars fall to the earth as figs fall from a
tree, the heavens roll out of sight, and sinners look
right up into the unveiled face of GOD, nothing
between! What do you think they're going to do? I'll
tell you. It will be the greatest prayer meeting this
world has ever had, but it will be *too late* to pray.

"**The kings of the earth, and the great men, and
the rich men, and the chief captains, and the
mighty men, and every [slave] and every free man,
hid themselves in the dens and in the rocks of the
mountains; and said to the mountains and rocks,
Fall on us, and hide us from the face of Him that sitteth on the throne, and from the wrath of the
Lamb**" (vv. 15,16). They are not repenting of sin. They
don't want to get right with God. They just want to
hide, for they don't want to meet Him!

Friends, there are people who would rather meet the
devil himself than to look in God's holy face. They shun
God. They run from God. They never run to Him; they
run away from Him. "Hide us from the face of God who
sitteth on the throne and from the wrath of the Lamb!"

Can the Lamb, our Lord Jesus, have wrath? We read of the wrath of God twelve times in Romans. What about the wrath of the Lamb Jesus? The One who died on the cross is angry with them. Wrath means anger. But don't you make that anything less.

I will never forget Dr. Hersey Davis, my professor when I was studying the Book of Romans in our senior Greek class in Louisville. The best notes I have on Romans are the notes that this dear man gave us in that class. When he came to the verse about the wrath of God being revealed from heaven against all ungodliness and unrighteousness, he said, "Young gentlemen, the wrath of God is God's settled hostility to sin and a sinful nature. He's got to stamp it out." And, beloved friends, God IS going to stamp out sin and all sinful nations the way you would crush a bug beneath your feet. There is no other way He can bring peace to this world. He has to get rid of sin. And He is going to do it. The wrath of God! The *orge* of God! We get our word "orgy" from that word. Chapter 6 ends with this statement: **"The great day of His wrath is come, and who shall be able to stand?"** (v. 17).

Chapter 7

Will People Be Saved During the Tribulation?

The Saved of the Tribulation

Will people be saved during the Tribulation? Chapters 6 through 19:11 tell about the Tribulation Period. "The Great Tribulation" is the term given to the second three and a half years before Christ returns, when God's intensified wrath is poured out on an unbelieving world. Will anyone be saved? Yes. It will be a time of great salvation. You say, "How can there be salvation when the Antichrist is sitting on the throne?" Well, God can do anything. There will be people who get right with God. One of the greatest revivals this world has ever known will occur during the Tribulation Period, in the sense of souls being saved.

Another question comes: "How can people be saved if the Holy Spirit has been taken out of the world?" He is not going to be taken out of the world. What the Bible says is, *"He that hindereth will hinder until He be taken out of the way"* (II Thessalonians 2:7). This means that the Spirit of God, who has been hindering, holding back sin, will then move to one side and let the sin of the world come to a head. Nobody has ever been or will be saved without the influence of the Holy Spirit of God, and He will be saving souls during the Tribulation.

"And after these things I saw four angels standing on the four corners of the earth, holding the four winds of the earth, that the wind should not blow upon the earth, nor on the sea, nor on any tree" (v. 1). The four corners of the earth. When I first started preaching, people laughed at this passage of Scripture, saying, "The Bible is scientifically untrue. The earth is round; it doesn't have any corners." But did you know that during the Geophysical Year scientists intensively studied this earth. And they said (without alluding to this Scripture) that the earth has *four corners.* It is not a perfect sphere. So don't be too concerned when somebody ridicules the Bible in disbelief. The Word of God is far ahead of science. It will be proven true. The God of the Bible cannot lie.

The four angels were standing on the four corners of the earth, holding the four winds of the earth. Here is angelic activity again, seeing to it that the wind should not blow on the earth, nor on the sea, nor on any tree. God controls the weather.

"And I saw another angel ascending from the east, having the seal of the living God: and he cried with a loud voice to the four angels, to whom it was given to hurt the earth and the sea, saying, Hurt not the earth, neither the sea, nor the trees, till we have sealed the servants of our God in their foreheads. And I heard the number of them which were sealed: and there were sealed 144,000 of all the tribes of the children of Israel. Of the tribe of Judah were sealed 12,000. Of the tribe of Reuben were sealed 12,000. Of the tribe of Gad were sealed 12,000" (vv. 2-5).

And there were 12,000 each from the tribes of Asher, Naphtali, Manasseh, Simeon, Levi, Issachar, Zebulon, Joseph, and Benjamin. I can't go into detail, of course, about these various tribes. Suffice it to say that the idea some people have about England being the "lost tribes" of Israel is ridiculous. God knows where the lost tribes are.

Verse 4 says that 144,000 Jews will be sealed. It means that they will be saved and protected by God through the Tribulation Period until their witness is finished. This mention of the 144,000 Jews involves the whole Jewish picture, one of the longest studies in the Bible. Only a remnant of the people of Israel will be saved, and here is part of that remnant. Not only will they be saved, but they will preach God's Word, and their preaching will result in a whole multitude of Gentiles being saved during the Tribulation Period.

"After this I beheld, and, lo, a great multitude, which no man could number, of all nations, and kindreds, and peoples, and tongues, stood before the throne and before the Lamb, clothed with white robes, and palms in their hands" (v. 9). That suggests joy. And they cried with a loud voice, saying, "Look! We saved ourselves! We made it to heaven!" Is that what the text says? No. **"They cried with a loud voice, saying, Salvation to our God which sitteth on the throne and unto the Lamb."**

One of my friends, a Christian, was talking to a man the other day and said, "You know, I am a sinner." His friend was indignant. He said, "I'M not a sinner." Maybe we are not preaching what we ought to preach if any are saying, "I'm not a sinner." Or if they are not coming to church; or if they are not listening to what we have to say from God's Word. People up in heaven ascribe their salvation not to themselves but to God who sits on the throne and to the Lamb.

"And all the angels stood round about the throne, and about the elders and the four living creatures, and fell before the throne on their faces, and worshiped God" (v. 11). That is what worship is—adoration, prostration before Jesus. We haven't worshiped till we do that in our hearts. Jesus isn't physically in this room, where I can fall on my face before Him, but if He were, I'd do it. I can do it in my study or my prayer room. And I can do it in my heart.

"Saying, Amen. Blessing, and glory, and thanksgiving, and honor, and power, and might, be unto

our God for ever and ever [unto the ages of the ages]. Amen. And one of the elders answered, saying unto me, Who are these which are arrayed in white robes? and whence came they? And I said unto him, Sir, thou knowest. And he said to me, These are they which came out of the great tribulation" (vv. 12-14). Literally, in Greek, "the tribulation, the great one," meaning, I believe, the second three and a half years before Jesus comes to earth.

"And have washed their robes, and made them white in the blood of the Lamb. Therefore are they before the throne of God, and serve Him day and night in His temple: and He that sitteth on the throne shall dwell among them. They shall hunger no more, neither thirst any more: neither shall the sun light on them, nor any heat. For the Lamb which is in the midst of the throne shall feed them, and lead them unto the living fountains of waters. And here is a passage I love so dearly, and I'm sure you do, too: And God shall wipe away all tears from their eyes" (vv. 14-17). These are people, a great multitude, saved in the Tribulation Period, and they appear in heaven. They believed on Christ at the cost of their lives. The Antichrist killed them. "Where did this great crowd come from?" "They came out of the great tribulation." "How did they get up here?" "They washed their robes and made them white in the blood of the Lamb."

The Precious Blood

Now I want to close with one word. And I confess to you I don't know how to say it. I've never preached this the way I want to preach it. I never will. I've never heard anybody else preach it the way it ought to be preached. Maybe when we get to heaven Jesus will say it the way I want to hear it. What is the Most Precious Thing in all the universe? If I were to ask you that, what would be your reply? God's Word says that the most precious thing in the universe is the blood of His Son—our Savior, the Lord Jesus Christ! First Peter

1:18 says, *"We are not redeemed with corruptible things, such as silver and gold, but with the precious blood of Christ, as of a Lamb without blemish and without spot."* We are redeemed with His blood.

Let's go back to chapter 5, verse 11. The chills go up and down my spine when I read this: *"I beheld, and I heard the voice of many angels round about the throne and the four living creatures and the elders, and the number of them was ten thousand times ten thousand, and thousands of thousands, saying with a loud voice, Worthy is the Lamb that was slain."* If I were to climb up to heaven and say, "Heaven, tell me. What is the Most Valuable Thing in this world?" untold millions of angels, and the four living creatures and the twenty-four elders, and everyone in heaven would instantly say, "Worthy is the Lamb that was slain!" Heaven is astonished at the loving sacrifice of Jesus, God's Son, who died for sinners, taking their place on the cross, taking their judgment, so they could come to heaven.

The other day I received a letter from a man sick in body, who was also suffering the condemnation of his sins. He said, "Brother Hendley, I'm broken in body, mind, and soul. Write and tell me four things. Tell me how I can be *sure* of heaven. Tell me how I can have *peace* with God. Tell me how I can get rid of my *guilt*. Tell me how I can get rid of the *memory* of my sins."

That is what every person who thinks at all about realities wants to know. How can I be sure of heaven? How can I have peace wth God and meet Him without blame? How can I get rid of the guilt of my sins? How can I wipe out the memory of my sins and failures?

Do you know how I answered that dear man? I turned to this passage that I read to you a moment ago. I said, "Here is a great multitude of people in heaven. They were once sinners on earth, even as you and I, but they are in heaven, standing with joy and festivity before the throne, uncondemned, with peace in their hearts, with no guilt, and with no memory of past sins. How did they get that way?" *"They washed their robes and made them white in the blood of the Lamb."*

Ladies and gentlemen, the most serious question facing each of us here, and facing every human being, is: "What is the meaning of washing our robes and making them white in the blood of the Lamb?" Because that's what it takes to get to heaven! I want to get to heaven, and if I must wash my robes and make them white in the blood of the Lamb, how do I do it? It surely doesn't mean that when Jesus died on the cross God took a big basin and caught the literal blood in that bowl, and if I'm going to be saved from my sins I must climb into that bowl and wash in that literal blood of the Lord Jesus Christ.

It simply means, beloved, that you and I are to come as poor lost sinners to God's Book and hear Him tell us that when Jesus Christ died on the cross He laid every sin of my life and yours over on Him. Jesus paid for all of my sins. He wiped them out. They don't exist anymore. I was estranged from God, but Jesus took care of it for me. It is not what I can do, have done, or ever will do; it is what HE did in those hours when He hung from 9:00 in the morning until 3:00 in the afternoon, 6 bloody hours, with a crown of thorns on His head, the blood dripping; the spikes in His hands and feet, the blood dripping; the spear wound in His heart; the blood dripping. All of that was for you and me, in our place!

I am to come before God and say, "God, I am a sinner. You know that. I have sinned again and again, in thought, word, and deed. I'm a sinner by nature. I'm a sinner by choice. I have no right to heaven at all. I have no right to come and live with You. But You tell me in Your Book that You love me, and that Your Son loves me, and that Your Son was willing to go to that cross and with His own blood pay the price of forgiveness for my sin, which is death. I believe He died my death for me, and I am trusting nothing but what Jesus did on that cross for me, to bring me to heaven." When you believe in Jesus, and receive Him into your heart, He gives you eternal life. When He saves you, you are saved forever.

Chapter 8

Four Trumpet Judgments

Now we begin chapter 8, concerning the four trumpet judgments that occur after Jesus opens the seventh seal of the scroll. In this chapter there will be only four judgments out of the seven. When we get to chapter 9, we have the fifth and sixth trumpet judgments, intensifying in severity and horror as they move toward the seven bowl judgments. All of this is the day of God's fierce wrath being poured out upon an unbelieving world, the three and a half years before Jesus returns with His church to the Mount of Olives and establishes His kingdom.

Silence in Heaven

"And when He had opened the seventh seal, there was silence in heaven about the space of half an hour" (v. 1). Silence in heaven? I suggested to you that heaven is a noisy place. One of the wonderful things about the Revelation is that so much is made known to us about heaven. I am planning on going to heaven. There are two studies I've tried to make above all others. First, I want to know *what God is like,* the God I must meet when I leave this world. Second, I want to know *what sort of place* awaits me over there. I have studied intently about God and heaven. They should be, I think, the two chief studies of the human mind.

Heaven is a Noisy Place

Heaven is a noisy place, a place of many souls, singing, the playing of instruments, loud voices. I brought along my "Heaven" New Testament tonight. I get a Bible and mark it all up with a particular study. Then I get another one and write in it profusely with notes on another study. This Testament is the one in which I did an intensive study on Heaven. Let me show you why I say heaven is a noisy place.

Chapter 4, verse 1: "After this I looked and, behold, a door was opened in heaven, and *the first voice which I heard was, as it were, of a trumpet talking with me,* which said, Come up here, and I will show thee things which must be hereafter." That loud voice was the voice of Jesus telling John to come up to heaven.

Chapter 5, verse 11: *"And I beheld and heard the voice of many angels around the throne, and the living creatures and the elders, and the number of them was ten thousand times ten thousand, and thousands of thousands, saying with a loud voice, Worthy is the Lamb."* Here are millions of angelic beings, and other heavenly beings, who are shouting, "Worthy is the Lamb!" Can you imagine that? What if everybody in Atlanta got together tomorrow, and all at one given signal would shout at the top of their voices, "Worthy is the Lamb!" Well, here is all heaven doing that.

Then chapter 7, verse 2: "I saw another angel ascending from the east, having the seal of the living God. *And he cried with a loud voice* to the four angels, to whom it was given to hurt the earth and the sea, saying "Hurt not the earth, neither the sea, nor the trees, till we have sealed the servants of our God in their foreheads." There again is the noise of angels speaking.

Chapter 10, verse 1: "And I saw another mighty angel come down from heaven, clothed with a cloud, and a rainbow upon his head; his face was as though it were the sun, and his feet like pillars of fire." Verse 3: *"And he cried with a loud voice, as when a lion roareth."* Like an excited lion, roaring, going after its prey.

Chapter 11, verse 12: *"And they heard a great voice from heaven* saying unto them, Come up here. And they ascended up to heaven in a cloud, and their enemies beheld them." These are the two martyred witnesses. The Lord says with a loud voice, "Come up here," and they just rise up from the dead and move into heaven when they are called.

Chapter 14, verse 6: "And I saw another angel fly in the midst of heaven, having the everlasting gospel to preach unto them that dwell on the earth . . . *saying with a loud voice,* Fear God, and give glory to Him, for the hour of His judgment is come. And worship Him that made heaven, and earth, and the sea, and the fountains of waters." God sends this angel in mid-heaven to evangelize the world in the Tribulation Period. People will see him. People will hear from him the Word of God.

Chapter 16, verse 17: "And the seventh angel poured out his bowl into the air, and *there came a great voice* out of the temple of heaven, from the throne, saying, It is done." It is finished.

Chapter 18, verses 1 and 2: "After these things *I heard a great voice of much people in heaven,* saying, Hallelujah! Salvation, and glory, and honor, and power, unto the Lord our God." Here's all heaven at one time shouting the praises of God! Heaven is a noisy place! I don't know what the decibels are, but I believe they are going to be loud.

Chapter 19, verse 6: "And I heard, as it were, *the voice of a great multitude, and like the voice of many waters, and the voice of mighty thunderings,* saying, Hallelujah! For the Lord God omnipotent reigneth."

Verse 17: "And I saw an angel standing in the sun; and *he cried with a loud voice,* saying to all the fowls that fly in the midst of heaven, Come and gather yourselves together unto the supper of the great God." When God judges the armies of earth, He is going to invite all the birds around the world to come and feast on the flesh of these enemies who fought against the returning Son of God. The Lamb is going to win, friends! That is the theme of the Revelation.

Then chapter 21, verse 3: *"I heard a great voice* out of heaven saying, Behold, the tabernacle of God is with men, and He will dwell with them, and they shall be His people, and God Himself shall be with them, and be their God."

There we have seen a multitude of redeemed people playing on harps and singing the praises of the Lamb and the praises of God. We have seen mighty angels roaring like a lion. Heaven will have all of these sounds, but you know, we won't have to sleep. We won't get tired. We won't get weary. We won't need pills. We can stand the noise. It's going to be wonderful in heaven. I just thought you might be interested in that quick summary of what God says about sounds in heaven.

Silence for a Half Hour

Now, that points up "the silence" that we have here in chapter 8, verse 1. When Jesus opens the seventh seal, all of a sudden heaven quiets down for a half hour. Nobody plucks instruments. Nobody sings. No angel speaks with a loud voice. A solemn, profound hush falls upon every heavenly being — the Father who sits on the throne, the Lamb in the midst of the throne, the 24 elders round about the throne, the four living creatures, the seven spirits of God, and every being in heaven. Everything is profoundly quiet.

There is only one explanation, and that is that heaven stands aghast at these horrible judgments that God has to bring upon men in order to clean up the sin and chaos in the world. Remember, judgment is God's "strange" work, His strange act. God is essentially love, but love has to judge that which would destroy it or the object of its love. That's the reason, fundamentally, why God has to judge. This profound silence in heaven is because of the approaching horrible trumpet judgments.

The Tabernacle

"And I saw the seven angels which stood before God; and to them were given seven trumpets. And another angel came and stood at the altar, having a golden censer: and there was given unto him much incense, that he should offer it with the prayers of all saints upon the golden altar which was before the throne. And the smoke of the incense, which came with the prayers of the saints, ascended up before God out of the angel's hand. And the angel took the censer, and filled it with fire of the altar, and cast it into the earth: and there were voices, and thunderings, and lightnings, and an earthquake. And the seven angels which had the seven trumpets prepared themselves to sound" (vv. 2-6).

Now let's look in verse 3 at this angel who came and stood at the altar. Evidently this is the golden altar of incense, for he has a golden censer. He was given much incense to offer with the prayers of the saints upon the golden altar which was before the throne.

We have to keep in mind that there is a heavenly tabernacle. The tabernacle on earth was made by Moses according to the pattern of the one in heaven.

The Brazen Altar

You remember that Israel sinned against God. But He made a way whereby, through sacrifice, they could come into His presence. The way of sacrifice was laid out in the tabernacle in the wilderness. When the people approached God, they had to come to the outer court first, to the brazen altar of sacrifice. A Jew would bring a little lamb, put his hand upon the head of the animal, and confess his sins. Symbolically, his sins were transferred to the head of this innocent victim. The priest then took the little lamb, cut its throat, caught the blood in a basin, and sprinkled the blood round about the brazen altar. Then he took the little lamb's body, placed it upon that altar, and it was consumed in the fire. The smoke went up to God. The little body was reduced to ashes. The ashes were caught and taken away, put out of sight. This meant that the man's sins were completely put away, obliterated, destroyed.

The Laver

Then the priest went on to the laver, which was also in the outer court, to wash and be ceremonially clean before he went to the Holy Place and the Holy of Holies. Before he could enter them, he had to wash his hands and face with water from the laver. The laver was made out of the looking glasses (mirrors) of the women. One could see his own reflection in the laver. It is a picture of the child of God kept clean today by confession of sin and cleansing by the Word. The laver represents God's Word and the cleansing that comes to our souls from it. When the priest looked into the laver, the looking glass reflected the dirt on his face and hands, and water was there to wash it away. When you and I look into the Word of God, it shows up our sins. But there is cleansing through faith in the promises of the Word of God. You and I are priests. Jesus made us kings and priests unto God His Father. We seldom hear about the priesthood of the believer, but we are priests, and we have to bathe to be fit to go into the Holy Place and minister before the Lord. It is through the Word that we stay clean.

The Holy Place

After the priest had washed at the laver, he parted the first curtain (veil) and walked into the Holy Place. The tabernacle itself had two rooms or compartments. The entrance was on the east side. The first room was called the Holy Place, and from there the priest went into the Holy of Holies. The rooms were separated by a curtain. The priest couldn't go through that curtain except once a year on the Day of Atonement.

The Holy of Holies

The Holy of Holies was the place where God dwelt. It had the ark of the covenant, which was a chest overlaid with gold. It was called the mercy seat. In this chest were the Testimony (the Ten Commandments),

Aaron's rod that budded, and a pot of manna. That golden lid was the place of atonement, where the blood of sacrifice was sprinkled. Overarching the ark of the covenant were two angel-like figures called the cherubim. God said, *"There will I meet with you and commune with you."* I repeat, nobody could go through that veil between the Holy Place and the Holy of Holies, except the high priest, and then only once a year, with the blood and a censer. Smoke covered him as he walked in on the day of atonement and sprinkled the blood seven times on the golden lid. Then he walked out and blessed the people and said, "Your sins for the past year are forgiven you."

The writer of the book of Hebrews reminds us that Jesus Christ, by His once-for-all sacrifice of His own self, has canceled the need to do that every year. Praise God, our sins are forgiven once-for-all by the sacrifice of Himself.

The Work of the Priest

Let me go back to what the believer-priest did, to remind you of the beautiful symbolism of the tabernacle. After he had offered the sacrifice and washed in the laver, he went into the Holy Place, where there were three objects, or furnishings. There was a table where twelve small loaves were placed, representing the twelve tribes of Israel, and this was food for the believer-priest.

It is a picture of Christ, our food for our spiritual lives. One of the most profound studies in the Bible is in the 6th chapter of the Gospel of John. Beloved, meditate on it until you grasp the meaning of Jesus' words when He said, *"He that keeps on eating Me shall live because of Me."* Every day we have to "digest" Jesus and the wonderful truths about Jesus. When you are hungry, you go to the table and eat, and strength comes into your body physically. So also spiritually; as we meditate on what Christ is to us in the Word of God, strength comes into our souls. That is the way spiritual life is maintained in the believer. So the bread, or showbread as it is called, was the food for the believer-priest.

In that room also was the light of a seven-branch golden candlestick. There was no natural light, no window. It was completely dark except for the light of the candlestick, which represents the Holy Spirit illuminating our souls. The priest was not only feeding on Christ, but walking and ministering in the light of the Holy Spirit.

Also in that room was a golden altar. God had told Moses how to make this altar. It was holy. Nobody was to make any of these things for himself. They were only for the Lord; they belonged to the Lord. So the priest placed incense on that altar, and the smoke went up to God daily. It was a sweet perfume, a sweet fragrance, in the nostrils of God. That is a picture of Jesus Christ, who is God's delight. As we come to pray, we come through the intercession of the Lord Jesus. Our prayers are acceptable to God only because they are mingled with His perfections. Our imperfections are done away, and at the golden altar of incense we can approach God in prayer.

We have that here in Revelation 8:3. *"And there was given him much incense, that he should offer it with the prayers of all saints upon the golden altar which was before the throne."* The book of Exodus tells us about the golden altar of incense, a picture of Christ interceding for us and our prayers going up to God together with Christ's intercession.

You see, we are not alone when we pray, beloved. The Holy Spirit is there. God's Word says in Romans 8, *"The Spirit maketh intercession for us, with groanings which cannot be uttered."* When I go to my prayer room, I know that my prayers are weak. I have often heard people say that you cannot sin in the prayer room. I disagree. If we examine our hearts, we will find sin there. When people minimize sin, I know they are not very close to God. The closer we get to God, the more we see sin in ourselves. The more we see Christ, the sinless One, the more we are aware of our sinfulness. Our acceptance before God is all because of Christ. It's all in the Lord Jesus.

Exodus 30

Exodus 30:1 says, *"Thou shalt make an altar to burn incense."* Verse 3, *"Thou shalt overlay it with pure gold."* Verse 6, *"Thou shalt put it before the veil [curtain] that is by the ark of the Testimony, before the mercy seat that is over the Testimony, where I will meet thee."* Verse 7, *"Aaron shall burn sweet incense thereon every morning."* The priest was to offer incense on the altar, and the smoke arising from the incense is a picture of the perfections of Jesus. When you and I come in prayer to God daily, in the perfections of Jesus, that is, when we pray in His holy name, it is like a sweet fragrance to God.

Verse 8, *"And Aaron lighteth the lamps, that he shall burn incense upon the altar morning and evening, a perpetual incense before the Lord throughout your generation."* Verse 9, *"You shall offer no strange incense thereon."* Prayer to God, without coming in Jesus' name, is an abomination to the living God. Whoever would honor the Father must honor the Son!

My wife and I were in the grandstands watching a Georgia Tech football game one day at Grant field. A man went to the loudspeaker and offered a prayer. He didn't say one word about Jesus. Louise looked at me and said, "That one didn't get through, did it?"

Beloved, did Jesus say, "If you ask anything, I will give it to you"? No. He said, *"If you ask anything in My name, the Father will give it to you."* That's the perfume. That's the sweet incense. That's the perfection of Jesus. When I come to God in Jesus' name and say, "Lord, I am not worthy even to be in Your presence, or for You even to look upon me, much less talk to You in prayer and ask You for things and get things from You, but I come in the merits of Jesus," the One in whom You delight, the One of whom You said, 'This is My beloved Son in whom I am well pleased' "—when I come in His name, my prayer gets through! It is accepted at the throne of God. HE is the sweet fragrance to God."

Notice the incense in Exodus 30:34. This is what Christ is to God. *"And the Lord said unto Moses, Take thee sweet spices."* Verse 35: *"Thou shalt make it a perfume."* God likes the sweet smell. This is the picture of God delighting in the perfections of His own Son. *"Tempered together pure and holy."* God loves purity. God loves holiness. Hebrews 1:9, *"Thou lovest righteousness and hatest iniquity. Therefore God, Thy God, hath anointed thee with the oil of gladness above Thy fellows."* Jesus is absolutely holy. He never said anything wrong, or thought anything wrong. He is the Father's delight.

Beloved, the beautiful thing is that we are accepted "in the Beloved." As He is accepted, so are we. The Bible says that when we accept Jesus as our Savior, the Father loves us just as He loves His Son. He loves us with the same love! One of the most amazing statements in the Bible is in I John 4. As Jesus in heaven is the delight of the Father's heart, so are we in this world. Yet millions of people in this world think that God will accept them apart from Jesus Christ! What an awakening, when they come to realize that no one comes to the Father but by HIM, and that He and the Father are One! The world is going to mourn one of these days when they find out what a horrible mistake they made about the Lord Jesus Christ.

In Exodus 30:37 God says, *"And as for the perfume which thou shalt make, ye shall not make to yourselves according to the composition thereof. It shall be unto thee holy for the Lord."* That is what Jesus is to God the Father.

Let's come back now to Revelation 8:3. There was given to this angel *"much incense, that he should offer it with the prayers of all the saints."* So the only way God can answer a sinner's prayer (and we are all sinners), or a believer's prayer, is that they be mingled with the incense of the perfections of Christ. When we come to God with that fragrance, God answers our prayers. Do you see what it means to pray in the name of Jesus? The phrase "In Jesus' name, Amen" means far more than just closing words of a prayer, as many people think.

First Trumpet

Let's go on now to the trumpet judgments. In the remainder of chapter 8 we have the first four trumpets, and they are terrible beyond words.

"The first angel sounded [the trumpet], and there followed hail and fire mingled with blood, and they were cast upon the earth: and the third part of trees was burned up, and all green grass was burnt up" (v. 7).

Let me pause for a minute and ask you a serious question. Do you believe the Bible? Do you really believe the Bible? The other day a woman I know was talking with a man who is a member of the church she attends. They were talking about Balaam's donkey speaking and forbidding the madness of the prophet. My friend is a Bible believer, a godly woman. This man sneered and said, "Nobody can make a donkey talk!" And he's a deacon in the church. No wonder some churches are spiritually cold, when their leaders are unbelievers. This man does not believe what God says! God says He made the donkey talk. It would be pitiful indeed if we had a God that *couldn't* make a donkey talk! So I ask: Do you really believe the Bible? To believe in God is to believe in miracles.

The *National Geographic* had a long article about the human cell. Your brain just reels to read about the discoveries of science. That little DNA molecule has the entire human being programmed in it, the entire plan of how tall you're going to be, the color of your eyes, and all the rest of your being. The kind of person you are going to be is in every one of those little DNA molecules. But do you know what these scientists said when they stood in awe of the research they had made? One said that the manner in which parents transmit their likeness to their offspring is as great a *mystery* as the lightning flash used to be to the savage in the woods. Another man said, quoting Winston Churchill, "It is a riddle wrapped up in a mystery inside an enigma." Now, who made that DNA molecule? God. He can do anything. He is the great Creator.

Do you believe the Bible? Do you believe that God drowned the world in a great flood that overtopped the mountains, and that God snuffed out the life of every human being except for eight persons who were spared, and from whom we have all descended? Do you really believe that? Do you accept it because you were taught it as a child, or do you believe it because you believe GOD? Do you believe that God delivered the children of Israel out of Egypt? Do you believe that God turned Lot's wife into a pillar of salt? Do you believe that a prophet by the name of Jonah was swallowed by a big fish that finally disgorged him on land, after which Jonah went and preached in the city of Nineveh?

Do you believe that God protected Daniel in the lions' den so that Daniel could say, "My God has stopped the lions' mouths"? Was it so? Did it actually happen? Do you believe that three Hebrew young men were flung into a fiery furnace seven times hotter than usual, and that when they were in that furnace they were so perfectly and absolutely protected by God that when they came out there wasn't even the smell of smoke on their garments? And yet when the men who cast them into the furnace fell in themselves, they were burned to a crisp? Do you really believe that God made the sun stand still, while He gave victory to Joshua?

Do you really believe that Jesus Christ was born of a virgin, that He was conceived by the Holy Ghost in the body of a virgin girl? Do you believe that Jesus died on the cross and rose from the dead on the third day? Do you believe that He is alive right now at God's right hand? Are you a believer? Most people are not. Most people in this world believe that the Bible is partly myths and fairy tales. I say to you that this Bible is a supernatural Book! Have you read it? Have the people who criticize it taken the time to study it? I'm not talking about this hop-skip-and-jump kind of reading. Have you read the Bible through, again and again and again? Have you taken any one of its books and read it through, again and again and again? Have you carefully studied its great themes, again and again and again? Have you opened your heart and mind and LET GOD SAY TO YOU what He wants to say?

When we come to these judgments, beloved, let's just believe God and take them for what they say. In your reading of books about the Bible, you will find that some writers say one thing and others say another. Take the Bible literally, unless you are forced to believe, from the context or elsewhere, that a particular verse is symbolic. These judgments in Revelation are literal judgments.

Second Trumpet

"And the second angel sounded [the trumpet], and as it were a great mountain burning with fire was cast into the sea: and the third part of the sea became blood" (v.8). God will turn one third of the oceans into blood in the Tribulation. Do you believe that? Do you believe that the Nile River in Egypt was turned into blood in the days of Moses? If God did it then, He can do it again. "And the third part of the creatures which are in the sea, and had life, died; and the third part of the ships were destroyed" (v. 9).

Third Trumpet

"And the third angel sounded, and there fell a great star from heaven, burning as it were a lamp, and it fell upon the third part of the rivers, and upon the fountains of waters: and the name of the star is called Wormwood: and the third part of the waters became wormwood; and many men died of the waters, because they were made bitter" (vv. 10,11).

Fourth Trumpet

"And the fourth angel sounded, and the third part of the sun was smitten. [The light is going out, friends.] And the third part of the moon, and the third part of the stars; so as the third part of them was darkened, and the day shone not for a third part of it, and the night likewise" (v. 12).

"And I beheld, and heard an angel flying

through the midst of heaven, saying with a loud voice, Woe, woe, woe, to the inhabiters of the earth by reason of the other voices of the trumpet of the three angels, which are yet to sound!" (v. 13).

Judgments! And the three yet to come will be worse than any that came before. God's wrath poured out upon an unbelieving world! More than 1900 years ago, God gave His Son to die for the sins of the world, sent His Spirit into the world, and sent witnesses over this earth to proclaim Jesus' name. Today, most people in this world couldn't care less. Sunday nights, churches (if open at all) are only half-filled. Where are the people? By their television sets, or out visiting one another, or somewhere else, but not gathering with God's people to hear the Word of God.

Chapter 9

The Fifth and Sixth Trumpet Judgments

Now we come to chapter 9 and the fifth trumpet judgment and the first woe.

"And the fifth angel sounded, and I saw a star fall from heaven unto the earth, and to him was given the key of the bottomless pit" (v. 1). This "star" is a mighty angel. He is given the key of the *abussos,* which means "a great deep, a bottomless pit." The Greek says, "the well of the pit." It has a mouth. It has a lock on the mouth. It has an opening, and then it spreads out into a deep. The word "abyss" is used of the depths of the ocean, which in some places is 8 miles deep.

"And he opened the bottomless pit; and there arose a smoke out of the pit, as the smoke of a great furnace; and the sun and air were darkened by reason of the smoke of the pit.

"And there came out of the smoke locusts upon the earth: and unto them was given power, as the scorpions of the earth have power. And it was commanded them that they should not hurt the grass of the earth, neither any green thing, neither any

tree; but only those men which have not the seal of God in their foreheads" (vv. 2-4).

Here is the Lord letting loose hellish, demonic locusts upon people, not to kill them but to torture them. Demons out of hell! You may say, "Well, that's allegorical." But if so, what are you going to make it mean? That is why many people go astray in their Bible study. Take the Word literally. God is going to send an angel to open up the pit and let loose these demons, these fallen angels, and they will torment people.

"And to them it was given that they should not kill them, but that they should be tormented five months. And their torment was as the torment of a scorpion, when he striketh a man" (v. 5). These locusts are not the little green insects that ravish whole areas of greenery, stripping it bare, as happens in the East—you've read about them. These are hellish locusts out of the depths of the pit. They will be let loose in the Tribulation Period to torment people.

"And in those days shall men seek death, and shall not find it: and shall desire to die, and death shall flee from them" (v. 6). Although people will want to die, they will not be able to commit suicide. No deaths, no funerals, for 5 months, 150 days. These hellish demons will prey upon the unbelieving who are not sealed by God, who have rejected the Lord. They will be unspeakably tormented.

"And the shapes of the locusts [notice] were like unto horses prepared unto battle; and on their heads were as it were crowns like gold, and their faces were as the faces of men. And they had hair like the hair of women, and their teeth were as the teeth of lions. And they had breastplates, as it were breastplates of iron; and the sound of their wings was as the sound of chariots of many horses running to battle.

"And they had tails like unto scorpions, and there were stings in their tails: and their power was to hurt men five months. And they had a king

over them, which is the angel of the bottomless pit,
whose name in the Hebrew tongue is Abaddon
[which means Destroyer], but in the Greek tongue
hath his name Apollyon [which also means
Destroyer]" (vv. 7-11).

It is the devil himself, the king over demons! Somebody says, "Are demons real?" The Bible says demons
are *real.* This isn't the only place where the Word
teaches us about demons. This is the Tribulation
Period, but in Mark 5 we read about a man in whom
were 6,000 demons. Jesus delivered the man, and the
demons entered 2,000 hogs and were driven into the
sea, where they were drowned.

In the foregoing passage we read that for 5 months
people will not be able to die. I call your attention to the
fact that life is in the hands of God. People will not be
able to jump out of hotel windows or take an overdose
of sleeping pills to get rid of these demons! Brother,
when God begins to judge, I don't want to be around. (I
won't be—I'll be in heaven with Jesus.)

Sixth Trumpet

Next, the sixth trumpet. Verse 13. Here we read of
the greatest army that ever has been or ever will be
assembled. It will be composed of 200 million hellish
horsemen.

**"And the sixth angel sounded, and I heard a
voice from the four horns of the golden altar
which is before God, saying to the sixth angel
which had the trumpet, Loose the four angels
which are bound in the great river Euphrates"** (vv.
13,14). The Euphrates River is literal. These angels are
literal. They are bound there because they are
destructive. These angels out of hell are going to kill at
least a billion people. But notice that they are bound
until the time comes. God controls hell. Don't forget
that, beloved.

Somebody said to me one time, "I get frightened
when you preach like this. You scare me." Every once
in a while someone will tell me that. But if you know

God, and know you know God, you need not be afraid.
You don't have to be afraid if you know that God is sovereign and that you are right with God. He will take
care of His own. But unsaved people ought to be afraid.

**"And the four angels were loosed, which were
prepared for an hour, and a day, and a month, and
a year, for to slay the third part of men. And the
number of the army of the horsemen were two
hundred thousand thousand [that's 200 million]:
and I heard the number of them"** (v. 16). There are
two ideas about this. One is that this is a human army.
But I cannot believe it because of the description beginning with verse 17:

**"And thus I saw the horses in the vision, and
them that sat on them, having breastplates of fire,
and of jacinth, and brimstone (sulphur): and the
heads of the horses were like the heads of lion; and
out of their mouths issued fire and smoke and
brimstone. By these three was the third part of
men killed, by the fire, and by the smoke, and by
the brimstone, which issued out of their mouths.
For their power is in their mouth and in their tails:
for their tails were like serpents, and had heads,
and with them they do hurt"** (vv. 17-19). Do you
know any army like that? I don't. Some commentators
say that this represents a modern army, the fire and
brimstone representing our modern tanks and planes
and rockets with their firepower. If these men want to
believe that, it's all right. But I will take it literally
unless I have to take it some other way. If we speculate
on it, we could have as many interpretations as we have
people.

Some years ago, people laughed at this Book of the
Revelation because they said nobody could ever field
an army of 200 million men! Do you know that today
China alone can field an army of 200 million people?
But I don't think that is what God is talking about.
Why would He go to all the trouble of telling us about
these strange, hellish horsemen, these monsters let
loose on men? Every time I hear or read about mon-

sters, I think about this chapter. For these are monsters, 200 million hellish horsemen, who will kill one third of the people of the earth.

We have already had in chapter 6 one-fourth of earth's population killed. Today the world population is over 4.5 billion, and the projection is that by the year 2000 (because of the population explosion) it will be 6 billion. But let's say, for the sake of illustration here that it is 4 billion. Chapter 6 says one-fourth of the people on earth will die; that is one billion. Here are the remaining three billion, and one-third are killed. That is another billion who die in these judgments. And there are other judgments also, all the way through this book, where people die. God will shut the heavens and there will not be a drop of rain for three and one-half years. That means famine. God will turn the waters into blood. People can't drink, and they will die right and left.

As I said before, earthquakes such as we have never known will rock the earth, and lives will be lost. I have made a study of earthquakes in the Bible, and, friends, I wonder about the earthquake era we are moving into now. Is this increase of earthquakes the beginning of the earthquakes the Lord is speaking about here? The Tribulation Period will begin with an earthquake, will continue with earthquakes, and end with an earthquake that will rock the cities of the earth to ruins in seconds! God is going to rise and shake mightily the earth! You have seen a picture of Atlas with the earth on his back. God is going to have the earth in His strong hands! And He is going to shake it! You see, beloved, this world has kicked up its heels in rebellion against God. But it is not always going to be that way.

Somebody may ask, "Why does God allow these judgments? Preachers tell us that God is a God of love. If He is, how can He let loose such horrible things on the human race?" There is only one answer: that more souls may be saved! God knows that for souls to go to hell is so horrible that He will do anything in the world to turn them around.

"And the rest of the men which were not killed by these plagues yet repented not of the works of their hands" (v. 20). There is the secret. That's why God sends judgment. God sends judgment to try to get people to repent. We have read in chapter 7 that some men will. There will be a great multitude of people saved during the Tribulation Period because of these judgments. God is always trying to get people to repent. First, God in love sends the sweet Gospel. He sends His Son to die for our sins. He sends the Holy Spirit. He gives us His Word at great cost. He sends us messengers, prophets, apostles, evangelists, pastor-teachers. But what do most people do? Pay little or no attention, so He brings a heavier judgment. And He keeps on. All of these judgments increase in intensity from the very first seal judgments, through the trumpets, and through the bowls, until God is literally going to shake the earth. He's going to clean it up. He's got to do it. But He will get some souls out of it.

They repented not of the works of their hands: **"that they should not worship demons, and idols of gold, and silver, and brass, and stone, and of wood: which neither can see, nor hear, nor walk: neither repented they of their murders"** (vv. 20,21). Murderers are walking the streets of Atlanta today unapprehended. They are in cities all over the world, but God knows every one of them. If you think God is not going to punish these murderers, you don't know God.

"Nor of their sorceries." In the paper it is not uncommon to read of people who are witches. Witches' covens are increasing all over the land. **"Nor of their fornication."** Awful sexual immorality is rampant all over the earth today. Do you think God doesn't know what is going on? Do you think God is going to condone it? **"Nor of their thefts."** They repented not! So God must bring greater judgment.

Chapter 10

The Towering Angel and the Little Book

We come now to chapter 10. This is another parenthetical chapter.

"And I saw another mighty angel [literally in Greek, strong angel] come down from heaven, clothed with a cloud: and a rainbow was upon his head, and his face was as it were the sun, and his feet as pillars of fire: and he had in his hand a little book (scroll) opened: and he set his right foot upon the sea, and his left foot on the earth, and he cried with a loud voice, as when a lion roareth: and when he had cried, seven thunders uttered their voices."

"And when the seven thunders uttered their voices, I was about to write: and I heard a voice from heaven saying unto me, Seal up those things which the seven thunders uttered, and write them not. And the angel which I saw stand upon the sea and upon the earth lifted up his hand to heaven, and sware by Him that liveth forever and ever, who created heaven, and the things that are therein, the earth and the things that are therein, that there shall be time [delay] no longer: but in the days of the voice of the seventh angel, when he shall begin to sound, the mystery of God should be finished, as He hath declared to His servants, the prophets" (vv. 1-7).

All through this book there are angels. There are good angels and bad angels. We have read about the bad angels from the Euphrates River who will kill 200 million people. But this is a good angel. He is a mighty one! If you ever need a bodyguard, ask the Lord to send this mighty angel to go along with you! He'll take care of all your enemies. He's big, and he's strong. Some people believe this is Christ, but I'm sure it can't be Christ, from studying other passages in the book. He is so big he is clothed with a cloud. He has a rainbow for a hat. His face shines like the sun. He is so big that he puts his right foot on the sea and his left foot on the land. He has a little open book (scroll) in his hand. He raises his other hand to heaven. When he roars, as a lion roars, suddenly seven thunders utter their voices. Do you believe the Bible? Do you believe that thunders can speak a language that can be understood? John heard these thunders talk, and he was about to write down what they said.

Verse 4 says that there came a voice from heaven saying, "Stop, John. Don't write what those thunders said." What did the thunders say? I don't know. Since we were not to know, it is none of our business. The best thing to do is leave it alone.

Then it is said that this mighty angel raised his hand to heaven and swore by God who lives unto the ages of the ages, who made everything in heaven and earth and under the earth, that there should be delay no longer. No more time. The familiar song "When the trumpet of the Lord shall sound and time shall be no more" comes from this verse. There shall be time no longer. Literally, there shall be delay no longer. From this point, God is going right on through with His judgments and clean up the world. All the unsaved will go to the lake of fire, and all the redeemed into the new heavens and new earth and the Holy City. God is not going to wait any longer.

All over Atlanta, people are living in sin that God abhors and hates as much as He hated the sin of Sodom and Gomorrah. Why doesn't He burn Atlanta to the ground as He did those two cities? Because we are living in the hour of grace. God alone knows the moment of His determination when the Rapture will take place. When the last person believes in Christ, completing the church, the church will be caught up to meet the Lord in the air. Then the hour of God's wrath will come upon the earth.

Verse 7: **"But in the days of the voice of the seventh angel, when he shall begin to sound, the mystery of God shall be finished, as He has declared to His servants the prophets."** You may be a Bible student. You love the Word and love the truths of the Bible. You love to study a theme. Here is one for you! The Mysteries of God. The Greek word *musterion* means "mystery, or secret."

God has some secrets. There's the secret of the kingdom in Matthew 13 and the great parables, the secret of Israel as the olive tree in Romans 11, and the secret of Christ and His church in Ephesians 3. The church is not in the Old Testament; it is hidden, a secret, something new that has been revealed through God's apostles in the New Testament. Then there is the secret of godliness in I Timothy 3:16, which is Christ, and the secret of the Rapture of the church: *"Behold, I show you a mystery [a secret]; we [Christians] shall not all sleep [die], but we shall all be changed, in a moment, in the twinkling of an eye, at the last trump: for the trumpet shall sound, and the dead in Christ shall be raised incorruptible, and we shall be changed."* We will receive our glorified bodies and be forever with the Lord (I Corinthians 15:52). There is also the secret of sin, or lawlessness, in II Thessalonians 2. And here in Revelation we have the mystery of God's wrath coming to an end.

I have just made a series of tapes on these different subjects of God's secrets that are now revealed to His people. If God is telling secrets, I want to know what they are! They are secret only in the sense that you must be born again to be able to understand what God has to say. *"For the natural man receiveth not the things of the Spirit of God. They are foolishness to him, neither can he know them, for they are spiritually discerned"* (I Corinthians 2:14).

Now at this point when the angel raises his hand and swears that there will be no more delay, John hears a voice.

"And the voice which I heard from heaven spoke to me again, and said, Go and take the little book which is open in the hand of the angel which standeth upon the sea and upon the earth. And I went unto the angel, and said unto him, Give me the little book. And he said unto me, Take it and eat it up. It shall make thy belly bitter, but it shall be in thy mouth sweet as honey. And I took the little book out of the angel's hand, and ate it up; and it was in my mouth sweet as honey: and as soon as I had eaten it, my belly was bitter. And he said unto me, Thou must prophesy again before many peoples, and nations, and tongues, and kings" (vv. 8-11).

We are not told what that little book contains. The Greek calls it *biblaridion,* "a tiny book." It contains the future judgments, the bowl judgments that finish the wrath of God and culminate in the most horrible things that can happen to human beings. John ate the book and it was sweet to his taste but bitter to his stomach. God is moving forward to a peaceful world: that is sweet. But He has to judge the world to do it: that is bitter. We are going to rejoice in the Holy City wherein dwells nothing but righteousness. Therefore, God cannot have unrighteous people there. That involves judgment. That is bitter. So in the Bible there are bitter things and sweet things.

Chapter 11

The Two Witnesses Killed and Resurrected

The Temple

Now as we come to the 11th chapter, we have two witnesses for the Lord in the city of Jerusalem. That is right in the middle of the Tribulation Period.

"And there was given to me a reed like a rod: and the angel stood, saying, Rise, and measure the temple of God, and the altar, and them that worship therein. But the court which is outside the temple leave out, and measure it not; for it is given unto the Gentiles: and the Holy City [Jerusalem] shall they tread under foot for forty and two months" (vv. 1,2).

This temple is the temple of the Antichrist in Jerusalem. Notice the time period: 42 months. That is three and a half years before Jesus comes to earth again. The temple will be rebuilt. The Jewish sacrifices will be reinstituted as part of the covenant the Antichrist will make with the Jews. But he will suddenly cause the sacrifices to cease, and he will set up his own image in the temple. He will set himself up as God.

Verse 2 says that the court outside is not to be measured, for it is given to the Gentiles. I don't know how many of you are Jews. I presume that most of us are Gentiles. But one of the great problems over the years has been the problem of the Jew and the Gentile.

The Wall of Partition

In ancient times, Gentiles were on the outside, excluded by the Jews. In the Old Testament period, the Gentiles didn't have anything and the Jews had everything. They had the patriarchs, the prophets, the Holy Scriptures, the promises, and the covenants. The Gentiles were on the outside. When the Jews built their temple, a place to worship God, they had a court for the women, but the court for the Gentiles was outside the temple proper. In Herod's temple, there was actually a 5-foot wall erected. A Gentile could come to that wall, but he dared go no farther under pain of death. Archaeologists have found a stone with the inscription of that death warning. It says that if a Gentile were to pass that wall and go inside, he would die. But Jews could go inside that beautiful temple and go through all their ritual and worship of God, with all the joys and delights of feast days. The Gentiles were walled out. The Jews had everything; we Gentiles had nothing.

But Jesus came! And when He died on the cross, He made *all of us* near to God through the shedding of His blood. He broke down the wall of partition. That is what Paul was talking about to the Gentiles in Ephesians 2:11. *"Wherefore remember, that ye being in time past Gentiles in the flesh, who are called Uncircumcision by that which is called the Circumcision in the flesh made by hands."* The Jews thought that God loved only them and didn't love the Gentiles. The Jews were given the rite and ceremony of circumcision, a mark in the flesh signifying that they were the people of God, were in covenant relationship with God, and had God's favor and blessing. The Jews were called Circumcision. The Gentiles did not have that mark, so they were called the Uncircumcised, or Uncircumcision.

Paul continued, *"That at that time ye were without Christ, being aliens from the commonwealth of Israel,*

*and strangers from the covenants of promise, having no
hope, and without God in the world."* Till Jesus came,
we Gentiles were Christless, countryless, promiseless,
covenantless, hopeless, and Godless. That was our
condition. Consider what Jesus did for us Gentiles!

*"But now in Christ Jesus ye who sometimes were far off
[outside the temple blessings] are made nigh by the blood
of Christ."* He brought us in, brother! In their special
relationship to God, the Jews can go way back, but we
can't. We go back to the cross. That's as far back as we
can go. Jesus brought us everything we have! We
wouldn't be worshiping God and delighting in His
Word today if it were not for our Jesus, our Christ who
died on the cross for us. *"For He is our peace,"* between
Jew and Gentile! He *"hath made us both one."*

Back in the Old Testament times there were only
Jews and Gentiles. But now there is a third dimension:
His church. So there are three divisions in the human
race: Jew, Gentile, and Church. When a Jew believes in
Christ, he moves into the church. When a Gentile believes in Christ, he moves into the church. That is the
threefold division. Ephesians 2:14, *"He is our peace,
who hath made both one, and hath broken down the
middle wall of partition."*

The partition! Paul is alluding to Herod's temple, to
that wall 5 feet high, which the Jews said must keep
out the Gentiles, who they thought were outside the
range of God's blessings. They said, "You are heathen.
You can't come in here and worship with us. We're on
the inside; you're on the outside. If you come in, we'll
kill you." When Paul wrote that in Ephesians, it was
A.D. 62 and Herod's temple was still standing. That
wall was still there. Paul wrote this in faith, using it as
an illustraton of how Jesus broke it down *spiritually!*
And in A.D. 70, Titus the Roman general conquered the
city and broke it down *literally,* and it has never been
rebuilt to this hour. But evidently it is going to be
rebuilt during the Antichrist's reign.

Ephesians 2:15-22, *"Having abolished in His flesh the
enmity, even the law of commandments contained in*

ordinances; for to make in Himself, of the two, one new man [the church], so making peace; and that He might reconcile both [Jew and Gentile] unto God in one body by the cross, having slain the enmity thereby.

"And He came and preached peace to you who were afar off [Gentiles], and to them that were near [Jews]. For through Him we both [Jews and Gentiles] have access by one Spirit unto the Father.

"Now, therefore, ye [Gentiles] are no more strangers and foreigners, but fellow citizens with the saints, and of the household of God; and are built upon the foundation of the apostles and prophets, Jesus Christ Himself being the chief cornerstone; in whom all the building fitly framed together groweth unto a holy temple in the Lord; in whom ye also are builded together for a habitation of God through the Spirit."

I am saying to you, beloved, that we had nothing till Jesus came. When He came and went to that cross, He made it possible for every Gentile to walk as close to God as any Jew ever had. Praise His name!

The Two Witnesses

"And I will give power unto My two witnesses, and they shall prophesy a thousand two hundred and threescore days, clothed in sackcloth" (11:3). That is 42 months, or three and a half years. There is a debate whether they will do this the first or the second three and a half years. I believe it will be the latter, because of the terrible, intensified judgments that will take place. The heavens will be shut up for three and a half years, then these two witnesses will bring down fire from heaven on their enemies. That seems not to be during the first half, which is more or less peaceful because the Antichrist is seemingly supporting the Jews. He has made a covenant with them. He has not yet revealed himself as the Antichrist. So I believe it is during the second half that these two men will be witnessing for the Lord. Called *"olive trees"* and *"lampstands"* in verse 4, they will prophesy. They will talk about, and for, the Lord Jesus.

"And if any man will hurt them, fire proceedeth out of their mouth, and devoureth their enemies: and if any man hurt them, he must in this manner be killed. These have power to shut heaven, that it rain not in the days of their prophecy" (vv. 5,6). There will be no rain on this earth during their time, three and a half years before Jesus returns. Famine will stalk this earth.

"And have power over the waters to turn them to blood, and to smite the earth with all plagues, as often as they will" (v. 6). Do you believe this? Do you believe the Lord is going to give two men absolute exemption from any hurt in the city of Jerusalem, with the Antichrist ruling right there over the whole earth? Do you think these two men can kill their enemies, bring down fire from heaven, and shut the heavens so that there won't be any rain while they are prophesying and witnessing for the Lord? Do you believe that? I do! They are immortal till their job is done. Nobody can touch them.

"And when they shall have finished their testimony, the beast [the Antichrist] that ascendeth out of the bottomless pit shall make war against them, and shall overcome them, and kill them" (v. 7). God will allow the Antichrist to kill them when their job is done.

"And their dead bodies shall lie in the street of the great city, which spiritually is called Sodom and Egypt, where also our Lord was crucified [Jerusalem]" (v. 8). Spiritually, it is called Sodom and Egypt. God looks at cities spiritually. I wonder what He calls Atlanta. I wonder what He calls New York, and Berlin, and Tokyo, and Washington. Oh, brother! I wonder what God says of them spiritually. You see, God looks through spiritual eyes. When I hear people saying, "Oh, what a great city we have," I think, "God, what do You think about Atlanta?"

"And they of the people and kindreds and tongues and nations shall see their dead bodies three days and a half " (v. 9). Will God use television then? The Lord can miraculously do anything He wants to do. But even naturally, cameras can be focused on these dead bodies, and people all over the world can see them by way of satellites. We have world-wide television. The entire world shall see their dead bodies three days and a half.

"And shall not permit their dead bodies to be put in graves. [Indignity will be vented upon these two great prophets of God.] And they that dwell upon the earth shall rejoice over them, and make merry, and shall send gifts one to another, because these two prophets tormented them that dwelt on the earth" (vv. 9,10). That expression, "that dwelt on the earth," is used again and again in the Revelation. It speaks of unsaved people that are satisfied on this earth. There are two words for "dwell" in Greek, *paroikeo* and *katoikeo*. The first means "a temporary dwelling," and the second means "settled down on earth, a permanent dwelling." This is the second word. They are settled down on earth. I call them "earth-dwellers," because that is what the Greek word means. They are satisfied with earth. They don't want the God of heaven.

Personally, I am not satisfied with earth. I want something better than this earth. People all over this city are saying, "Just give me the pleasures of earth and time. You can have God and salvation and heaven."

Now because these people were "earth-dwellers," they felt tormented. How did the two witnesses torment them? I'll tell you. Goodness always torments badness. Godliness always torments ungodliness. This is the age-old conflict, friends. This is the battle still going on today, and it will continue to go on. There is much talk about people fighting one another ethnologically and militarily. But the greatest battle, the Bible says, is the spiritual conflict between godliness and ungodliness, between people who worship God and people who do not, between Christ and the devil. Do you know who's going to win? I do; I've read the last chapter of the Book! So the earth-dwellers make merry and rejoice when the witnesses are slain.

"**And after three days and a half the spirit of life from God entered into them, and they stood upon their feet; and great fear fell upon them who saw them. And they heard a great voice from heaven saying unto them, Come up here. And they ascended up to heaven in a cloud, and their enemies beheld them**" (vv. 11,12). Jesus went up in a cloud from the Mount of Olives. Literally, in Greek, "A cloud took up under Him and He rode back to heaven." These prophets of God rode a cloud back to heaven! At the Rapture (I Thessalonians 4:13), we're going to ride a cloud! I don't know what I'm going to do with Louise; she doesn't like airplanes much. But the Lord will take care of her.

Verse 13: "**And the same hour was there a great earthquake, and the tenth part of the city [Jerusalem] fell.**" Jerusalem under the Antichrist will be rebuilt with beautiful buildings, but one-tenth of the city will be rocked to ruins in this earthquake. "**And were slain of men seven thousand.**" Seven thousand people will die in that earthquake. "**And the remnant were terrified, and gave glory to the God of heaven. The second woe is past; and behold, the third woe cometh quickly.**"

Seventh Trumpet

"**And the seventh angel sounded, and there were great voices in heaven, saying, The kingdoms of this world**" (v. 15). Change the word "kingdoms," plural, to "kingdom," singular. One of the better translations has it in the singular. It reads literally, *"The kingdom of this world is the kingdom of our Lord and of His Christ, and He shall reign forever and ever."* The world kingdom belongs to Jesus! To One King!

Study the governments of this earth under sin. Men of different nations have said, "This is the best kind of government." Utopia, you know—perfect social and political life. Plato had his own idea about the best

kind of government. Monarchies and fascist governments have come and gone. Communism today has
swept over a major portion of this world. We have our
own idea of the best rule of human beings. I suppose our
kind of government has produced the greatest results
the world has ever known. But even with that, the
human race is still suffering, and will. "What we
need," someone has said, "is a beneficent dictator." We
have one, in Jesus! And He is coming again! "The kingdom of this world will become the kingdom of our Lord
and of His Christ, and He shall reign forever and ever."

**"And the four and twenty elders, which sat
before God on their seats, fell upon their faces,
and worshiped God"** (v. 16). We've found out what
worship is. It is the heart going out in prostration to
God, God being adored. We haven't worshiped if we
haven't adored God, loved God, ascribed to God the
praise and glory due His name.

**"Saying, We give Thee thanks, O Lord God Al-
mighty, which art, and wast, and art to come; because Thou hast taken to Thee Thy great power,
and hast begun Thy reign"** (v. 17). If God were to
take His great power tonight in this city, the population would be drastically lower before morning. In fact,
I'll tell you this. If Jesus Christ and God the Father
were to put in an appearance tomorrow at high noon
and begin to reign, there would be a great exodus from
this city. You see, by nature people don't love God. God
must get people converted or judge them, in order to
bring peace to the world. There is no other way.

When somebody tells me, "I don't like all of this," I
say, "How would you do it?" Suppose you, like God, had
promised the human race after the fall of Adam that
you would bring peace to this earth, paradise restored.
How would you restore paradise? Only two ways can it
be done: get everybody saved, or get them out of the
way. God in His great love and mercy sent Jesus the
first time to die on the cross for our sins. He provided
salvation for every human being who will ever be born.
But most people don't want Christ. Some of us do, but

the masses do not. They don't want Him around. That's why they won't go to church. That's why they won't read the Bible. That's why they won't pray. GOD is the Most Unloved Being in this universe! People drink in His goodness, and never so much as bow their hearts and give Him thanks and praise.

Verse 17: The twenty-four elders say, "Thou hast taken Thy great power." God is going to take His power one of these days. **"And the nations were angry,"** (v. 18). Angry at God! Read Psalm 2, where all the nations are banded together against the Lord and His Christ, saying, *"Let us break Their bands asunder; let us cast their cords from us. But He that sitteth in the heavens shall laugh. The Lord shall have them in derision. Then shall He speak to them in His wrath and vex them in His sore displeasure. Yet have I set My King upon My holy hill of Zion."*

When I was a young man, there were some people called "Post-Millenarians." They said, "The Gospel is going to get everybody converted and we're going to have a sweet Millennium here on earth, without Jesus. Everybody is just going to become nice and wonderful, without Jesus returning at all. He will come AFTER the Millennium." You don't hear much about that crowd now. All the while, the Bible said the opposite, that in the endtime the world would be in revolt against God and His Christ.

That is what we have right here in Revelation 11:18. The nations are angry! It agrees with the rest of the Bible. **"The nations were angry, and Thy wrath is come, and the time of the dead, that they should be judged"** (v. 18). Beloved, that passage teaches that everybody lives on. How are you going to judge a man if he is dead? The only way you can judge a dead man is for him to come alive. The time of the dead is coming when they will be judged.

"And that Thou shouldst give reward unto Thy servants, the prophets, and to the saints, and them that fear Thy name, small and great, [Listen, here is the key to it] **and shouldest destroy them which**

destroy the earth" (v. 18). Every human being born into this world is either constructive or destructive. One of the most pitiful sights is to see a man who has kicked up his heels and been destructive all his life. He lives 60 or more years and then gets converted. He realizes what a fool he has been. Oh, beloved, God is so wonderful to save him! But think of all the lost years, the wasted years, that cannot be relived!

"And the temple of God was opened in heaven." [This is the heavenly temple. The study of the "Temples in the Bible" is such a precious thing.] **"And there was seen in His temple the ark of His covenant: and there were lightnings, and thunderings, and an earthquake, and great hail"** (v. 19). Notice, the temple in heaven is open. That temple is the dwelling place of God Himself, open to all who come through the Lord Jesus Christ. If you have never come to God for salvation through personal faith in Christ, do it now. He will save all who call upon Him in truth, as promised in His Word.

Chapter 12

The Protection of Israel

This is the middle of the Tribulation Period, which is from chapter 6 through 19:11. Jesus is in heaven. He is removing the seals of the Book of the End. Out of the seventh seal come the seven trumpet judgments, and out of the seventh trumpet judgment come the bowl judgments. These are still ahead. As the Revelation progresses, between some of the judgments we find "parenthetical" passages that deal with special things supplemental and not necessarily chronological.

This chapter deals with the protection of Israel during the Tribulation Period. Only a remnant out of the people of Israel will be saved. The word "remnant" means "fraction." If you have not studied this word "remnant" in the Bible as it relates to Israel, by all means do so. If you have a Scofield Reference Bible, it will help you. If you do not, study the word from your Strong's Concordance. You can't study your Bible without a concordance! It will be a great blessing to you to trace the word "remnant" in the Word of God. The Bible teaches that only a remnant of Israel will be saved. The study of Israel in the Scripture is one of the most tremendous studies, in which we learn about God's promises and plans and purposes for Israel.

"And there appeared a great wonder in heaven [a great marvel, an astonishing thing], a woman clothed with the sun, and the moon under her feet, and upon her head a crown of twelve stars. And she being with child cried, travailing in birth, and pained to be delivered.

"And there appeared another wonder in heaven, and behold, a great red dragon having seven heads and ten horns, and seven crowns upon his head. And his tail drew the third part of the stars of heaven, and did cast them to the earth. And the dragon stood before the woman which was ready to be delivered, to devour her child as soon as it was born.

"And she brought forth a male child, who was to rule all nations with a rod of iron: and her child was caught up unto God, and to His throne. And the woman fled into the wilderness, where she hath a place prepared of God, that they should feed her there a thousand, two hundred and three-score days [1260 days]" (vv. 1-6).

Three personages are found in verses 1 through 6. The pregnant woman, the red dragon, and the newborn male Child whom the dragon is seeking to destroy. Without question, this woman is the nation of Israel: Israel gave birth to Jesus Christ. Our blessed Lord was born, according to the flesh, of the Jewish nation. We owe the Jews so much. Israel is the "great wonder." She is clothed with the sun, and the moon is under her feet. She has on her head a crown of twelve stars, symbolic of the twelve tribes of Israel. She is with child, travailing in birthpangs to be delivered.

Waiting to devour the child as soon as it is born is a great red dragon called "another wonder in heaven." The dragon has seven heads and ten horns. In this scene we have the whole teaching of God's Word from the birth of the Lord Jesus into the world, right down to the very end when the dragon will seek to destroy the people of Israel. The seven heads and ten horns represent the ten-kingdom alliance, the revived Roman Empire under the Antichrist, which will be the devil's instrument to try to destroy the Jews from off the face of the earth, before our Lord comes back to this world again.

The child is the Lord Jesus Christ, destined to become the ruler of all nations. Some have tried to make this woman the church. Some say this woman is Mary, the mother of Jesus. But it has to be the nation of Israel. As we go on, we'll see this confirmed.

"She brought forth a male child who was to rule all nations with a rod of iron." The iron-rod rule of Jesus is used a number of times in the Bible of His millennial reign. When He comes to this earth and reigns for a thousand years, He will have to reign with a rod of iron because there will be opposition. A rod is an instrument of authority, or of punishment. Our Lord will control the nations of earth in the Millennium, but it will require a rod of iron.

"Her child was caught up unto God and to His throne." That refers unquestionably to the ascension of the Lord Jesus Christ. From His very birth, Satan tried to destroy Him. Through King Herod, he tried to destroy Him. Herod, jealous of the Child he couldn't find, simply killed ALL the children up to 2 years of age. All through the Bible, Old Testament and New, are evidences that Satan was trying to hinder Christ from being born. Then, after His birth, Satan tried to keep Him from going to the cross to become the Savior of men. The devil hates God! He hates Jesus! He hates Israel! He hates the church of the Lord Jesus Christ! They all have a special place in God's plan. The devil is not a myth, but a very real being, and here he is called the dragon.

Notice verse 6: **"And the woman fled into the wilderness where she has a place prepared by God, that they should feed her there for 42 months."** That is exactly three and a half years, the latter half of the Tribulation Period when the Antichrist will be ruling over the earth. During this time God will protect Israel. God will have a place prepared for her in the wilderness. If the Lord had not protected Israel, she couldn't have survived. She would not be existing today, except for God's protective power. Right now there are nations that would like to obliterate the Jews from the earth. She has been and will be God's instrument, God's witness. In ancient times, she was God's witness in a heathen world. Twice in Isaiah 43 God said, "Ye are My witnesses, that I am God." When you study the hatred of the nations for Israel, this is the main reason. The devil fights God everywhere he can, and he fights the instruments of God.

Israel is the nation that gave us our Bible! Every writer except Luke is a Jew. The prophets were Jews. Our Lord Jesus Christ was a Jew. Beloved, when you take away what Israel has given us, we haven't very much left. She has given us the knowledge of God and of Christ through the Scriptures. Here is the devil seeking the final destruction of the nation of Israel.

Israel Trodden Down by Gentiles

I must turn aside to give you a quick sketch of Israel's history. Our Lord Jesus said, *"Jerusalem shall be trodden down of the Gentiles till the times of the Gentiles shall be fulfilled."* "The time of the Gentiles" means that period of time from Nebuchadnezzar's invasion of Judah, when he took Judah captive, until Christ's second coming to earth. Our Lord said Jerusalem would be trodden down. That is, the Jewish people would be under the dominion of aliens. The nations would be hostile to her. She would not have her own sovereignty but be under alien power, until the second coming of our Lord.

I remember June 1967, when the Six-Day War occurred. The Jews were able to take the city of Jerusalem from the Arabs. When I was in Jerusalem in 1955, the Wailing Wall was in the hands of the Arabs. The main holy places around Jerusalem were in the hands of the Arabs. When our plane touched down on a land-ing strip there in Jerusalem, I had to take my handbag myself and move from the Israeli side and go through the Vandenburg gate to the Arab side. Almost all the holy places of Israel were in the hands of the Arabs at that time.

But in the Six-Day War the Jews captured the city of Jerusalem for themselves, and they were in jubilation! I heard people say, "Jerusalem will never be trodden down again! She is free!" God's Word doesn't say that. It says she will be trodden down "until the times of the Gentiles be fulfilled," and I am sorry to say it.

Two years ago I was again in the city of Jerusalem. Dr. Daniels had a group of about 192 people, and he invited me to speak on Israel. I stood there in the King George Hotel and gave a lecture on Israel. Jewish people were all around me, but I had to paint this picture of Israel's future suffering. This nation has suffered like no other nation. She was trodden down by the Babylonians, trodden down by the Medo-Persians, trodden down by the Greeks, trodden down by the Romans (Israel was under the heel of Rome in the time of Christ), trodden down after she was dispersed among the nations, trodden down by the Moslems, trodden down by the Turks, trodden down by the Crusaders, trodden down by England (England had the mandate over Israel when she was trying to establish a homeland), trodden down by the Germans. Every time I think of it I shudder. Can you believe that Hitler murdered 6 million Jews in gas chambers, in an attempt to exterminate this nation? It is the most horrible blot on the human race.

In May of 1948, Israel was reconstituted a nation, after many centuries in dispersion. On that day my heart beat fast, because I knew from prophecy that God said He would bring her back into the land in unbelief.

And today what do we find? The Arabs are her enemies. She is surrounded by enemies that would like to destroy her. I heard Arab leaders say that they would drive her into the sea! They are out to destroy Israel utterly.

What about the future? God says in Ezekiel 38 and 39 that Israel will be invaded by Russia. A great power from the north of Palestine will invade the Holy Land in the endtime. But God will destroy those invading armies on the mountains of Israel!

She will be trodden down by the Antichrist. He will befriend her for the first three and a half years of the Tribulation Period, but in the latter three and a half years he will try to destroy every Jew he can. And that is where we are, here in chapter 12.

Finally, at the very end, all the nations will be gathered together against Jerusalem to battle (Zechariah 14:1). All nations will be out to exterminate the Jew. Not just three or four, but all nations of the earth will seek to destroy the Jews from the face of the earth. In that moment and not until then, under the pressure and threat of total extermination and without a friend in this world, Israel will turn and call upon Christ!

You remember when He was climbing toward Mount Calvary, struggling under the weight of the cross, some of the Jewish women along the roadside were weeping. He said to them, *"Don't weep for Me. Weep for yourselves and your children."* He was looking ahead down the centuries and seeing all this that I've just recounted to you, all the suffering and agony that Israel would go through. He was saying, "You think that I am going through agony? You don't know what you as a nation are going to go through." Then He said, *"You will not see Me henceforth until you shall say, Blessed is He that cometh in the name of the Lord."*

Today, Israel is still rejecting Christ as Savior and Lord. *"He came unto His own [to Israel, more than 1900 years ago], and His own received Him not."* They said, *"Away with Him! Crucify Him! We have no king but Caesar."*

But when these nations come against Israel, as God's Word says in Zechariah, two-thirds of the people in the Holy Land will die. But God said He would bring one-third through the fire. They will be refined as silver is refined. When the nations come to destroy Israel, then the Jews will turn to Jesus, whom they have repudiated all these centuries, as their Messiah and their Lord. Without a friend in the world, and facing extermination, they will call on Christ as their Messiah and Deliverer and say, *"Blessed is He that cometh in the name of the Lord."* In response to their cry, He will come the second time. His feet will touch down on the Mount of Olives from which He went up, and He will cause the Mount of Olives to split. Part of it will move toward the north and part of it toward the south for the escape of His people, and *"they shall look upon Him who they have pierced,"* whom they rejected when He first came in love. And they will mourn as a family mourns over the death of an only son because of their awful mistake of the centuries in rejecting Him. They will say to Him, *"The Lord is our God,"* and He will say, *"You are My people,"* and the new millennial nation, the true Israel, will be born in a day. That is the remnant that will be the holy seed, moving into the Millennium, to form the greatest nation this world has ever known! Israel, not another, will be the leading nation in the Millennium. This is clearly taught in the prophecies in the Word of God.

Suffering—Why?

Now the question comes, Why has this nation suffered as no other nation? Why has she been the target of the supreme enemy, the devil? Because she is God's witness to the nations. God didn't call Israel to wrap her self-righteous rags around herself and say, "God loves only me, and you Gentiles are without any promises, prophets, and covenants. You are outside the pale of God's blessing." God called her to be a witness to all nations. God called Israel to Himself, revealed Himself to her, gave her His Spirit and His Word, and finally gave her Jesus Christ her Messiah, that she might be a witness to the nations of the earth.

But she failed God. Today, still in unbelief, she rejects God's Son, her Messiah. (The church is doing almost the same thing today, according to Laodicea, which we studied in Revelation 3. The apostate church is headed for the same thing—failing God as a witness on this earth today.) So Israel failed to be the witness God planned her to be, and her supreme crime was that she turned her back on God's Son when God sent Him to her. *"He came unto His own, and His own received Him not."* But thank God, He turned to the Gentiles! The Scripture says, *"As many as received Him, to them gave He power to become the sons of God, even to them that believe on His name"* (John 1:12).

We gave that background so that you would better understand this chapter. Verse 6 says that the woman fled into the wilderness where God prepared a place for her, and she would be fed there for three and a half years. God will protect and preserve a remnant of Israel through the Tribulation Period. She will be converted when she sees Jesus at the end of the Tribulation Period, as I have described. That holy seed, that remnant, will become the nucleus of the new nation during the Millennium.

War in Heaven

"And there was war in heaven: Michael and his angels fought against the dragon; and the dragon fought and his angels, and prevailed not [the dragon prevailed not]; neither was their place found any more in heaven. And the great dragon was cast out, that old serpent, called the Devil, and Satan, which deceiveth the whole world: he was cast out into the earth, and his angels were cast out with him. And I heard a loud voice saying in heaven, Now is come salvation, and strength, and the kingdom of our God, and the power of His Christ; for the accuser of our brethren is cast down, which accused them before our God day and night" (vv. 7-10).

Here is that sinister being you don't hear very much about these days—the devil. And because he is not recognized, he is holding high carnival. So many of our young people are taken in by him because they don't know anything about him. I was preaching in Florida recently, where a group of churches came together and held a meeting in the auditorium. One night I preached on hell. I went back to my motel room and the telephone rang. It was a pastor friend of mine, and he said, "There is a young lady here who wants to speak to you." She came on the line. I could tell she had been weeping. She said, "I just want to thank you for preaching that message on hell tonight. I did not know it was so bad. Knowing that I was going to hell, I was so disturbed that I had to have some help. I couldn't go to sleep. So I called the pastor and asked him if I could see him. I went to his home, and he just led me to Jesus. Again, I want to thank you for preaching about hell. I didn't know it was so bad." What an indictment against many of us when young people have to say they haven't heard about hell! Beloved, there is a hell, and most people are going there. There is a devil, and he is deceiving people everywhere. In this passage are some of his names. He is called a red, fiery dragon. People laugh about that.

When I was in Singapore on the Communist side, I saw dragons all over the place. They say it is a mythological thing. I'll guarantee you that the devil isn't mythological. The name "devil" means "slanderer." He slanders God to you and you to God. He tries to keep you and God apart. The name "Satan" also means "adversary." You have an enemy, beloved! He's out to break you. If he can, he'll keep you from Christ so that he can have your soul! He knows he is going to hell, and his desire is to take as many people with him as he possibly can. But if you make up your mind you are going to believe on Christ and be saved, the next thing he will try to do is sabotage your life and keep you from helping anybody else to be saved. He is your enemy!

I am afraid that most of our Christian people today are asleep in the coils of the enemy and don't even realize it. For example, why is it so hard to pray? Why can you talk to a friend on the telephone for an hour and a half without stopping, but it is hard to pray for 10 minutes? Why can you read the newspaper, every word that's in it, and read books and magazines of this world that damage your mind and soul, but you can't sit down for a delightful study of God's Word for an hour? Why is it that you can talk volubly about almost any subject, but to tell somebody what Jesus means to you is the most difficult thing you've ever tried? And so you go day after day and week after week without witnessing. I'll tell you why. There is an adversary who is keeping you from these things! He will keep you from Bible study. He will keep you from prayer. He will keep you from witnessing.

This enemy came to the woman in the Garden of Eden. In Genesis 1, we read about God and Adam and Eve. Everything was wonderful. But in Genesis 3, when the devil stepped in—trouble! He came to Eve when she was alone and said, *"Yea, hath God said?"* He put a doubt in her mind about God's Word. If the devil can get someone to doubt God's Word, he can easily possess the soul. Multitudes of people today do not believe that the Bible is the Word of God; the devil has their souls. If you don't believe the Bible is the Word of God, he'll have your soul. The devil struck Job's health, wealth, children, wife, and everything he had. He stripped him absolutely down. He tempted David to number Israel when God had said, "Thou shalt not," and thousands of people in Israel died. He hindered the apostle Paul. Listen to me, Christian. I tremble when I remember this. Paul said, *"I would have come to you at Thessalonica, but Satan hindered me."* Paul was one of the greatest Christians, I think. There may be somebody else as great, but I cannot conceive of anybody else who lived for the Lord more devotedly than Paul. If the devil hindered him from doing the will of God on one occasion, how many times have we let the devil hinder us?

He wrestles with the church. Paul said, *"We wrestle not against flesh and blood, but against principalities, against powers, against rulers of the darkness of this world, against spiritual wickedness in high places"*

(Ephesians 6:12). It is a deadly wrestling match. I used to teach wrestling at the YMCA in Atlanta, and many times I have seen men pinned to the floor, flat on their backs, made totally helpless by their opponent. When I think about Christians today, how many are just pinned to the mat by the enemy, Satan! We don't realize we are in a deadly wrestling match.

The devil isn't physical. You cannot fight him with your fists, you can't shoot him with a gun, you can't stab him with a knife. But he is our enemy, far more deadly than any human enemy could be. He is called *"the deceiver of the whole world."* The reason Christians are a tiny minority is that the world is deceived by the devil. He tells them the way they are going is the way to go, instead of Christ's way. I'd like to remind you that he is not in hell. God's Word says, *"The devil is a roaring lion, walking about, seeking whom he may devour."* You don't see him with your eyes, but he is moving everywhere, influencing and inducing people to do wrong. Oh, how many young people, and older people, are being devoured by the devil today!

His kingdom is called "the kingdom of darkness." He is the ruler of this world system. God's Word says that the devil is the god of this age. What does he do? He is the tempter. One of the most profound studies in the Word of God is Matthew 4, where Satan comes to tempt our Lord. When you study it, you will find that he brings the same temptations to you. He will try to pull you away from God. He will try to cause you to stumble. He will try to break you. He will try to ruin you physically, mentally, and spiritually.

But the main thing the devil tries to do is wreck your faith in Jesus. On one occasion Jesus Christ turned to the apostle Peter and said, *"Simon, Simon, behold, Satan hath desired to have you, that he may sift you as wheat; but I have prayed for you that your faith fail not"* (Luke 22:31,32). The devil struck at Peter's faith! Many people are throwing their faith overboard.

I sat with a man who came to see me in a hotel in Kentucky. He said, "I'm a member of First Baptist

Church. My family doesn't know this, and please don't tell them, but I have no faith in God or Christ or the Bible or anything." I wouldn't be in that man's shoes for fifty million worlds. He told me he went to a school that is supposed to be a theological school, supposed to stand for God and the Bible, and his professors wrecked his faith. They blasted it to bits. That's why I ask, do you *believe?* Do you really believe this Bible? How much will you risk on that belief? There is a devil!

"And the great dragon was cast out, that old serpent called the Devil, and Satan, which deceiveth the whole world: he was cast out into the earth, and his angels were cast out with him" (v. 9). What does that mean? Did the devil have access to God in heaven? Yes. We learn that from the book of Job. The devil had access to God. As the accuser of the brethren, he accuses us before God day and night. Here he is cast out into the earth for his final fling. He will try to strike down the human race.

Somebody may be asking, "Why does God give the devil access to Himself? Why does God give the devil access to human beings? They must be tested. When you say, "God, I love You," He will test that love. When you say to God, "I have faith in you," God will test that faith. God tested Abraham, not with a temptation to immorality, but to put him to the test. When you say, "I am a believer in the Lord Jesus Christ," and "I love the Lord," God is going to have you prove it. I've had to prove it, and you will too. The devil will throw everything at you he possibly can; that is his business.

Satan is the accuser of the brethren before God day and night; that is the reason for Christ's intercession. When a Christian happens to do something wrong, the devil goes running to God and says, "Look at that Christian down there! He did something wrong! You are not going to bring him to heaven like that, are You? I demand punishment because he broke one of the laws, and when one is broken all are broken. The wages of sin is death. I demand the death penalty for that Christian." But the precious blood of Calvary covers that sin, and the Christian has the intercession of Jesus. He says, "Father, it is true that that Christian has just sinned, but look at these nail wounds. I have already paid the penalty for that sin." Oh, the grace of our God and Savior toward us poor sinners!

Verse 11 is one of the great verses of the Bible: **"And they overcame him [the devil] by the blood of the Lamb."** They believed God. Do you believe this Bible? Do you really believe that God has already punished every sin of your life, so that now He cannot justly punish you, because you believe in Jesus' atonement for you? Do you really believe your sins are gone? If so, you have peace about them. When people call me and say, "How am I going to get rid of this guilt? How can I get rid of the memory of my past sins?" I know they have never really believed what the blood of Christ, the Lamb of God, has done for them. They have never seen Jesus as their own substitute on the cross. Oh, they know it theoretically, but they've never really believed it. Has your heart ever rested in the finished atonement of Jesus? Have you ever really believed that all the punishment your sin deserved was meted out to Jesus on that cross? When you believe on Him, *"there is therefore now no condemnation to them who are in Christ Jesus"* (Romans 8:1). *"They shall not come into judgment, but [are] passed from death unto life"* (John 5:24).

"And by the word of their testimony." They were not afraid to testify for the Lord, even when their lives were in jeopardy. **"And they loved not their lives even unto the death."** They were totally surrendered to God. They were willing to die rather than be untrue to Jesus.

"Therefore rejoice, ye heavens, and ye that dwell in them. Woe to the inhabiters of the earth and of the sea! for the devil is come down unto you, having great wrath, because he knoweth that he hath but a short time" (v. 12). The devil is cast out of the presence of God in heaven and down to the earth in the last three and a half years of the Tribulation. He has only a short time in which he can operate.

"When the dragon saw that he was cast unto the earth, he persecuted the woman [the woman is Israel], who brought forth the male child [Christ]. And to the woman were given two wings of a great eagle, that she might fly into the wilderness, into her place, where she is nourished for a time, and times, and half a time, from the face of the serpent" (vv. 13,14). Hebrew scholars tell us that in the Hebrew language "a time" means a year. "Times," plural, means two years. "Half a time" means a half year. So that adds up to three and a half years. That agrees with the prophecy in Daniel: 1260 days or three and a half years, or 42 months.

"And the serpent cast out of his mouth water as a flood after the woman, that he might cause her to be carried away of the flood. And the earth helped the woman, and the earth opened her mouth and swallowed up the flood which the dragon cast out of his mouth" (vv. 15,16). There is Satan seeking to destroy Israel the last three and a half years before Jesus comes again. But God in grace protects her, even though she has not yet believed. She doesn't believe in Christ until He returns. Isaiah said, *"The Redeemer shall come out of Zion and turn away ungodliness from Jacob [Israel]."* Israel is not converted until the Lord returns. But she is protected by God. She is a holy seed and she is going to be saved. God in His wonderful knowledge knows all things from the beginning to the end. The foreknowledge of God is a very precious study. Everything is as clear to Him in the future as though it were the present. So He protects Israel, the Jewish remnant.

"And the dragon was [angry] with the woman [Israel], and went to make war with the remnant of her seed, which keep the commandments of God and have the testimony of Jesus Christ" (v. 17). That is the protection of the nation of Israel during the Tribulation Period.

Chapter 13

The Rise of the Antichrist

When the church is caught up to meet the Lord in the air, the Marriage Supper of the Lamb and the Judgment Seat of Christ will take place in heaven. Meanwhile, the Tribulation Period will break on earth. It will be so terrible that Jesus said if it were not cut short by His return, no human life would be left on this earth. There will be worldwide war, worldwide famine, worldwide pestilence. Then the Antichrist is coming, an awful, fearful being who will rule this world in hellish power for three and a half years before the Lord Jesus Christ comes again.

In the book of Daniel, chapter 7, God gave the prophet a vision of the endtime and of four great world kingdoms that will precede the coming of Christ to establish the kingdom of God. The first kingdom was like a lion, the second like a bear, the third like a leopard, and the fourth like an indescribable monster. The four successive kingdoms were Babylon, Medo-Persia, Greece, Rome. The fourth kingdom, the Roman Empire, was like a wild beast with ten horns. Those ten horns are very important. Daniel explains them in 7:24.

The ten horns are ten kings. This is the ten-kingdom alliance of nations arising out of the Roman Empire, in Europe and around the Mediterranean Sea, that will furnish the power for the reign of the Antichrist for the latter three and a half years of the Tribulation, the seven-year period between the Rapture of the church (I Thessalonians 4:13-18) and Christ's return to the Mount of Olives (Revelation 19:11-15). Not Russia, not the United States of America, but Europe will be in the saddle of authority and power under the reign of the Antichrist. After the first three and a half years, the Antichrist, with the power that this ten-kingdom alliance will give to him, will be ruling this world in absolute authority. Nobody will be able to challenge him.

We read further in Daniel 7:24, *"And another shall rise after them* (the ten kings)." First, the forming of the ten-kingdom alliance, and then "another" shall rise. This is the Antichrist. *"He shall be [different] from the first, and he shall subdue three kings. and he shall speak great words against the Most High, and wear out the saints of the Most High and think to change times and laws. And they shall be given into his hand until the time and times and the dividing of time."*

This is the first identification of "the man of sin," the Antichrist. Not many years ago some people thought that one of our world leaders at that time might be the Antichrist. But the Antichrist cannot come until this ten-kingdom alliance out of the Old Roman Empire is formed. Today we have the European Common Market composed of ten nations, but a ten-kingdom military alliance is coming.

First, it will be formed. Then an eleventh power comes up, and the leader subdues three of the original ten. This is the first identification of the Antichrist. He will make a covenant with the Jews. Daniel 9:27 says that he shall confirm the covenant with many (the Jews) for one week, meaning a "week of years," a seven-year period of time.

Jesus said to the nation of Israel, *"I have come in My Father's name and you receive Me not. When one comes in*

his own name, him ye will receive." He was speaking of
the Antichrist. When the church is caught up to meet
the Lord, Israel will make a covenant with Antichrist
for a seven-year period divided into two equal
segments. The first half will be somewhat peaceful. He
will be protecting the Jews and gaining in military and
political power. But when he reaches the zenith of his
power, which is in the middle of the seven years, he will
tear off his mask and proclaim himself to be God. He
will be revealed to the world as the Antichrist, the man
of sin, the man of lawlessness, and will seek to kill all
who refuse to worship him. He will rule this world in absolute power and authority for the latter three and a
half years, until a final rebellion of all the nations
occurs at the end of the seven years, at the second
coming of our Lord Jesus Christ. The man of sin will
rule this world! He will get what Hitler did not get,
what Napoleon did not get, what Alexander the Great
did not get—absolute authority over the world!

The Beast (Antichrist)

Here in the 13th chapter of the Revelaton we find
some of the details of his life. In verse 1, John says,
**"And I stood upon the sand of the sea and saw a
beast rise up out of the sea."** The word "sea" means
the Gentile nations. Here is one reason I believe the Antichrist will be a Gentile, not a Jew. Some people think
that because he is called "the son of perdition" (a lost
soul), as was Judas Iscariot, the Antichrist also will be
a Jew. But he comes up out of the "sea," the nations.

John saw "a beast." The Greek word is *therion,* "a
wild beast." There are two kinds of beasts, one domes-
ticated like the cow, and the other wild like the lion.
"Having seven heads and ten horns." This is the ten-
kingdom alliance that will first be formed, then the
Antichrist puts down three. *"And upon his horns ten
crowns, and upon his heads the name of blasphemy."*
This word "blasphemy" means "to speak lightly or pro-
fanely of divine things," here speaking against God
and the things of God and the people of God.

Verse 2: **"And the beast which I saw was like unto a leopard, and his feet were like the feet of a bear, and his mouth like the mouth of a lion: and the dragon gave him his power, and his seat, and great authority."** You will find the leopard, the bear, and the lion in the passage in Daniel 7. This alliance of nations in that day will have the characteristics of these wild beasts.

From heaven's standpoint, the kingdoms of the earth are like wild, ravenous, rapacious, cruel animals. Man talks about how great the human race is, but when God looks down upon the kingdoms of earth He sees them as wild animals. That's what heaven thinks about us! We have to live in the Bible to think as heaven thinks. We must stay in God's truth. If we are constantly reading things that are of earth, we'll think earthly; if we read the things of God's Word, we'll think heavenly.

Verse 3: **"And I saw one of his heads, as it were wounded to death; and his deadly wound was healed: and all the world wondered after the beast."** Many students of Bible prophecy believe that this is the restoration of the imperial rule of the Caesars. Rome has never really ceased to exist in spirit. God's Word bears that out. For the fourth wild animal (the Old Roman Empire) continues with ten horns in his head until the very end, when it is destroyed. A great Roman ruler is coming, just before the Antichrist, which we'll find in chapter 17. Rome will be revived. That will be the deadly wound that was healed. The nation itself will come alive. This ten-kingdom alliance out of the Old Roman Empire will be revived. Verse 3 tells us that all the world will be astonished at this ten-kingdom alliance with its tremendous power.

Verse 4: **"And they worshiped the dragon."** Here is the whole world (except those who are born again) worshiping the devil! They worshiped the dragon, **"which gave power unto the beast (the Antichrist): and they worshiped the beast, saying, Who is like unto the beast? Who is able to make war** with him?" This means that nobody will be able to make war with him. Nobody on earth can resist him.

Verse 5: **"And there was given unto him a mouth speaking great things and blasphemies [against God]; and power was given unto him to continue forty and two months."** That is exactly three and a half years. This exact time period runs all through the Book of the Revelation and the Book of Daniel.

"And he [the Antichrist] opened his mouth in blasphemy against God, to blaspheme His name, and His tabernacle, and those who dwell in heaven." Remember, at this time the church isn't here on earth; the church is in heaven with the Lord. The whole world is worshiping the devil, and the devil's man is controlling this entire world and blaspheming God to the top of his voice.

Verse 7: **"And it was given unto him to make war with the saints, and to overcome them."** These saints (godly people) are not the saints of the church age. There were saints in the Old Testament, there are saints in the church age, and there will be saints in the Tribulation Period, which are the saints we have here. If we do not discern this, we get into trouble in interpreting the Word of God. So he will make war with the saints of the Tribulation Period and overcome them. Many Christians will die.

"And power was given him over all kindreds, and tongues, and nations." Language cannot be more specific as to the absolute rule of the Antichrist. **"And all that dwell upon the earth shall worship him, whose names are not written in the Book of Life of the Lamb slain from the foundation of the world."** All people who are not converted to Christ will worship the Antichrist as God! This world will have rejected God and His Son. **"If any man have an ear, let him hear."** People who are spiritually capable of understanding this, let them understand.

Verse 10 speaks of **"the faith and patience of the saints,"** whom the Antichrist is persecuting.

Now verse 11. The Antichrist will have a false prophet to proclaim him. This world has seen many false religions. Some religions have swept over the world, and you wonder how people could ever believe in them. In my travels, I have found multitudes of people who reject Christ as their Savior. They believe in God, but according to the Bible, they will not be saved, because nobody comes to God except through Christ! *"No man cometh unto the Father, but by Me,"* said Jesus. God says there is no other way. Any religion that does not come to God through Christ is false. Many people are being deluded by false religions. But the greatest of all false religions will appear three and a half years before Jesus comes again, and its leader will be this false prophet. He will persuade all the world (except people whose names are in the Lamb's book of life) to worship the Antichrist instead of Jesus.

"I beheld another [wild] beast coming up out of the earth; and he had two horns like a lamb, and he spoke like a dragon. And he exerciseth all the power of the first beast before him [Antichrist], and causeth the earth and them which dwell therein to worship the first beast, whose deadly wound was healed." More than once we have the mention of a "deadly wound." A deadly wound is one that kills. It causes death. And when it is "healed," it means resurrection from the dead. Many expositors do not believe this, even though they admit that a deadly wound must mean a wound that causes death. I respect them, but I cannot get away from this language. The Antichrist, killed, is going to rise from the dead. That is why the whole world is going to believe he is God! There has not been an authentic resurrection since Christ! If Lenin, who has been lying in state all these years in Russia should suddenly stand up, and by way of television the whole world would see him walking around again, with everybody knowing that this man was indeed the same Lenin, now alive from the dead, it would be the most shocking event ever seen! That is exactly what is going to happen to the Antichrist.

Now let's read about the prophet of the Antichrist in

verse 13. **"He doeth great wonders, so that he maketh fire come down from heaven on the earth in the sight of men."** He can walk out in the street and pull down columns of fire in the presence of the people. This is not make-believe; he actually does it by Satanic power. Verse 14: **"And deceiveth them that dwell on the earth by the means of those miracles which he had power to do in the sight of the beast."**

This word "miracle" is the same word used of Jesus' miracles. But these are inspired of Satan. When you hear somebody today proclaiming himself to be a miracle worker, look out, brother. God's Word says it is possible for a person to preach, to cast out demons and do miracles, and yet go to hell! (Matthew 7:22,23.) Our Lord in the Sermon on the Mount said that in that day when people stand in His presence, some will say to Him, "We prophesied. We cast out demons. We did many wonderful works." But He will say to them, "I never knew you. Depart from Me, ye workers of iniquity." Today, if somebody does what seems to be a miracle, multitudes go flocking after him. Look out! That is what the Antichrist is going to do.

So the false prophet had this power to do miracles in the sight of the wild beast, **"saying to them that dwell on the earth that they should make an image to the beast, which had the wound by a sword, and did live. And he had power to give life unto the image of the beast."** This false religious leader will have the power to give life to the image of the Antichrist. It doesn't say that this is a robot. The word for "life" here is "breath" in Greek. He actually gives breath to the image! It breathes.

God is going to allow this. People who will not believe God, not believe His Word, not believe the truth, shall be deceived. Second Thessalonians 2 says that God will send them *"strong delusion that they should believe [the lie that the Antichrist is God], that they all might be condemned who believed not the truth but had pleasure in unrighteousness."* God means for His Book to be believed! There are two absolute truths, Christ and the

Bible. Jesus said, *"I am the truth,"* and *"Thy Word is truth."* When people turn away from Christ and the Bible, they turn away from absolute truth to deception.

The false prophet will have power to give life to the image of the beast, **"that the image of the beast should speak, and cause that as many as would not worship the image of the beast should be killed."** The image will breathe. The image will speak! This is not ventriloquism. **"And he causeth all** [all whose names are not in the Book of Life], **both small and great, rich and poor, free and bond, to receive a mark in their right hand, or in their foreheads, and that no man might buy or sell except he that had the mark, or the name of the beast, or the number of his name."** Without his mark, nobody can carry on commerce or have a job. People can't live without food, so if they are in this society they have to go along with the Antichrist or die. For the first time, man will control the world by computers.

Verse 18: **"Here is wisdom. Let him that has understanding** [the word translated "understanding" is the Greek word "mind"] **count the number of the beast [the Antichrist]."** It is not the number of a system or of a false church. **"It is the number of a [devil-inspired man], and his number is six hundred three score and six."** That is 666.

Somebody may ask, "Who is the Antichrist?" I do not know. Many believe that the Roman emperor Nero Caesar will be the Antichrist. One of the reasons is that when the name Nero Caesar is spelled out in the Hebrew letters it yields the number. Nero was one of the most wicked human beings in all history. His life made such an impression on the early church that many believed he would be raised from the dead and become the Antichrist. However, many other names have been suggested. One thing is certain. The coming Antichrist will be the most gigantic personality ever to walk across the stage of human history. He will persuade the world to worship him instead of Jesus Christ.

Chapter 14

The 144,000 on Mount Zion With the Lamb

In chapter 14 we have the Lamb on Mount Zion with the 144,000. "And I looked, and lo, a Lamb stood on Mount Zion, and with Him 144,000, having His Father's name written in their foreheads. And I heard a voice from heaven as the voice of many waters, and as the voice of a great thunder: and I heard the voice of harpers playing upon their harps: and they sang as it were a new song before the throne, and before the four living creatures, and the elders: and no man could learn that song but the 144,000, which were redeemed from the earth. These are they which were not defiled with women; for they are virgins. These are they which follow the Lamb whithersoever He goeth. These were redeemed from among men, being the first-fruits unto God and to the Lamb. And in their mouth was found no guile [literally, no lie]: for they are without fault before the throne of God."

Who are these 144,000 who are with the Lamb? In chapter 7 we saw that they are Jews who will be sealed by God during the Tribulation Period. God will protect them; otherwise the Jewish nation would be destroyed. God will seal 12,000 out of each tribe. So 144,000 Jewish people will be saved during the Tribulation period. Here they are on Mount Zion with Jesus. Mount Zion is Jerusalem. Jerusalem is built on several hills, such as the Mount of Olives; Mount Moriah, where the temple area is; Mount Ophel, which was the original Jerusalem; and Mount Zion, which was David's place and finally came to mean all of Jerusalem. In this Scripture we are not told who these 144,000 people are who stand with Jesus on Mount Zion. We believe, and many commentators believe, that they are the same 144,000 sealed in chapter 7. If they were sealed by God at the beginning of the Tribulation, they went through it faithful to the Lord and preaching the Word, resulting in a great multitude of Gentiles being saved.

Description

They have the Father's name written in their foreheads. God stamps them as His own. All believers will have that, as we'll see at the close of the Revelation.

Notice also the purity of these people. Verse 4: *"These are they which were not defiled with women; for they are virgins."* We know that immorality and obscenity are prevalent in this day in which we live. There are sections of our newspapers that the godly must pass over because they are defiling to the mind. There are television shows Christians will not look at, books they won't read, and entertainments they will not go to. God says, "Whatsoever things are true, honest, just, pure, lovely, and of good report, think on these things." If our minds think on the garbage and iniquity of this world, that's the kind of minds they are going to be. But the immorality today is almost nothing compared to the depravity that will be on this earth in the Tribulation Period when the devil's Antichrist will be in authority, totally against God and His Word and Christ and Christians, with the whole world worshiping the devil's man and the devil himself. You talk about corruption? This world will be a cesspool of iniquity during the Tribulation. But these 144,000 come through all the immorality with purity!

We learn next that *"they follow the Lamb whithersoever he goeth."* They have communion with Jesus. They walk with Christ in purity in the midst of this awful impurity. They follow not the world but Christ the Lamb!

I made a study of the Greek word "follow" one time, and it was one of the richest blessings I ever had. The Greek word is *akoloutheo,* and it means "walking the same road with someone." When Jesus passed by and said to those fishermen by the Sea of Galilee, "Come, follow Me," what He said was, "Come and live with Me. Come, let's be companions every day, not just seeing each other once a week. Follow Me. Let's share life together. Be My companion. Let's walk together every day." Of course, these men had their homes, but they were with Jesus every day. They walked with Christ. So may we.

Continuing verse 4, *"These were redeemed from among men, being the firstfruits unto God and to the Lamb."* The word "redeemed" (as mentioned before) means "to buy." They were "bought" from among men by the blood of the Lord Jesus. They believed in His blood atonement for their sins. "And in their mouth was no guile," no lie. They were truthful. And "without fault before the throne of God." Literally, "without blemish." The Greek word *momos* means "a spot." If I get a spot on my coat but I send it to the cleaner, when it comes back it will be a *amomos,* "without spot." Sacrificial animals in the Old Testament had to be without spot, free of flaws, to be offered to God. Christ, by His death for these people, made them fit for the presence of God. So also we today are children of God, without blemish by faith in Him.

Beloved friends, aren't we reminded of what John tells us in his first epistle? "He that has this hope [of seeing Jesus and standing in His presence at the Rapture or at death] purifies himself." He is continually purifying himself, even as Christ is pure. Our Lord holds up before us, as our goal, His absolute purity. Even though we will not attain to that perfection in this world, that is to be our goal. *We shall be like Him, for we see Him as He is.* Until then, we should be striving for more and more purity in thought, word, and deed. "More like the Master," we sing, "I would ever be."

The Angel Evangelist

Next, in verse 6, we have the angel evangelist. If you could get this angel to come and preach for you, you'd be doing real well! In the Tribulation Period, God is going to send an angel to evangelize the earth, but not with the same message we are preaching. **"And I saw another angel fly in the midst of heaven, having the everlasting gospel to preach unto them that dwell on the earth, and to every nation, and kindred, and tongue, and people, saying with a loud voice [here is his gospel], Fear God, and give glory to Him; for the hour of His judgment is come; and worship Him that made heaven, and earth, and the sea, and the fountains of waters."**

Now, we'll understand this when we translate it, "having the eternal good news." The word "gospel" means "good news." This angel is not preaching the gospel of the reconciliation; he is preaching the gospel of judgment, the good news about judgment, the good news that God is judging the world. How can that be good news! It's good news because the result of judgment will be a perfect world. "We look for a new heavens and a new earth where dwelleth righteousness." So all people and things not right with God will be destroyed. Then only will this world have peace. This angel is announcing the good news that God through judgment is moving on to that perfect world! What good news that is!

In verse 8 the fall of Babylon is announced, but the actual fall doesn't occur till the 18th chapter. Here it is announced ahead of time. Constantly in the Bible you find what some commentators call the Law of Recurrence. God will make a statement, and later He will give the fulfillment. For example, in the Book of Genesis mention is made of man's creation but not in detail; a later chapter goes into detail. God does that time and again in the Word. Verse 8: **"And there followed another angel, saying, Babylon is fallen, is fallen, that great city, because she made all nations drink of the wine of the wrath of her fornication."**

Doom

Now we come to one of the most terrible statements in the Bible: verses 9-12. Simply stated, any person who receives the mark of the Antichrist is instantly doomed for hell. **"And the third angel followed them, saying with a loud voice, If any man worship the beast and his image, and receive his mark in his forehead, or in his hand, the same shall drink of the wine of the wrath of God, which is poured out without mixture into the cup of his indignation; [listen] and he shall be tormented with fire and brimstone [listen] in the presence of the holy angels, [listen] and in the presence of the Lamb, and the smoke of their torment ascendeth up unto the ages of the ages: and they have no rest day nor night, who worship the beast and his image. And whosoever receiveth the mark of his name."**

They will be tormented with fire and brimstone. Some people don't believe in torment. I have in my study a book by a very well-known Bible teacher, a man I always thought was one of the most honest men with the Bible. Lo and behold, toward the end of his life he denied that there is any such thing as torment. When I read that, I went to my Greek Testament and checked the Greek word *basanois*. It is in the plural. *"The rich man died and was buried, and in hell he lifted up his eyes being in torments"* (Luke 16). "Torture" is the meaning of the word. Here it is again in the Revelation. People are being tortured. Don't ask me to explain it, I can't. But the Bible wouldn't tell us this if it were not so!

Years ago we pitched a large tent across the street from our church for the purpose of having evangelistic meetings. But at the last minute our evangelist was unable to come. I made no pretense of being an evangelist. I was a pastor. All I had ever dreamed of doing was just studying the Bible and trying to teach it to anyone who would listen. It turned out that I had to do the preaching in the tent meeting. So every day I would shut myself up in my room and dig out some truth from God's Word for the evening service, and I would go to the tent each night and pour it out.

One day I spent a whole afternoon studying Luke 16. "The rich man died and was buried, and in hell he lifted up his eyes, being in torments." I took my Testament and carefully studied every aspect of that passage. I checked every word, every phrase, every sentence, every paragraph. And, beloved friends, when I came out of my study that day, I knew I lived in a world of people *going to hell.* That conviction has driven me for all these years, and it continues to drive me. We are in a world of lost souls! God says that people are going to hell. I don't understand it, but it's the teaching of the Word of God. It's all through the Word of God! And the person who said more about it than anyone else was Jesus, the One who died to keep people out of hell.

"Tormented with fire and brimstone." Where? *"In the presence of the Lamb."* These people who worshiped the Antichrist will be tormented in the presence of God's holy angels and in the presence of the Lamb. Listen to me. Jesus did all He could do. He died to save them. Can you imagine tormented souls, tortured souls, looking up into His face and seeing the nail wounds in His hands and the marks on His forehead, realizing *too late* what He did for them? Can you imagine that agony?

A man told me the other night about witnessing to another man about Jesus. The response? "I don't believe. I don't believe in heaven or hell. I went to Seminary to study to preach, but now I don't believe in heaven or hell." When he comes to die, it will be a different story.

My older brother didn't believe in heaven or hell either. He claimed to be an atheist. He believed that

when people die they are just like the dogs or cats or
chickens—they're dead. For 47 years I prayed for him.
One day he had a stroke. I cried to God about my lost
brother. I was in agony. I said, "Lord, all these years
Joe has refused my testimony. Lord, is my brother
going to *hell?* I have been warning people everywhere,
telling them that there is a hell. I have seen multitudes
of souls believe on Jesus and escape hell. Now is my
own brother going to hell?"

Well, Joe, who had resisted me all those years, actually called for me! When I walked into his room, he
said, "Pray for me." What a change of heart! Within a
few minutes, I led him to Christ! As long as the blood
was flowing in his veins and he had money in his pocket
and had his loved ones around him, he could deny God
and the Bible, heaven and hell. But oh, when you come
down to *the end,* and you are stripped of everything,
and you're in a nursing home, and your loved ones can
visit you only now and then, and your sight is gone, and
your heart is bad, and you suffer a stroke, and you
know you are *dying,* going into eternity, it's a different
picture. Whenever I hear some smart aleck say that he
doesn't believe in God or the Bible or heaven or hell, I
think, "Go ahead, brother. The day is coming when you
will believe! I just hope you will receive Christ before it
is forever too late."

Verse 11: *"And the smoke of their torment ascended up
forever and ever."* That phrase "forever and ever" is
used of God's existence; He lives forever and ever.
"Unto the ages of the ages," literally. It is also used of
the eternality of the believer; we shall live forever and
ever with God. It is used also of the judgment of the
lost; they shall be tormented unto the ages of the ages.
So as long as God lives and the saved are with him in
heaven, lost souls are going to be tormented in hell, for
the same phrase is used of all three: the unendingness
of the life of God, the life of the saved, and the existence
of the lost.

Verse 12 mentions again the patience and obedience
of the saints in the time of persecution, and verse 13

says, "I heard a voice from heaven saying unto me,
**Write, Blessed are the dead which die in the Lord
from henceforth: Yea saith the Spirit, that they
may rest from their labors; and their works do
follow them."** You have heard in funeral sermons,
"Blessed are the dead who die in the Lord," but those
two words "from henceforth" are left out. Now, I am
not saying that the speaker should not use this verse,
because people who die in the Lord are indeed blessed.
But that isn't the meaning of it in this passage. This is
during the Tribulation Period, and the bowl that is
filled with God's wrath is about to be poured out. It
means, "To die will be a blessing," because the people
will escape these awful judgments about to come on the
earth. It will be better to be dead than to suffer these
judgments.

Finally, the judgment of Christ is announced. Verse
14: **"I looked, and behold a white cloud, and upon
the cloud one sat like unto the Son of man."** That
is Jesus. All judgment is committed into the hands of
the Son. **"Having on His head a golden crown, and
in His hand a sharp sickle."**

Verse 15: **"And another angel came out of the
temple, crying with a loud voice to Him that sat on
the cloud, Thrust in Thy sickle and reap, for the
time has come for Thee to reap; for the harvest of
the earth is ripe."** This reminds us of the parable of
the wheat and tares in Matthew 13. When Jesus comes,
He will separate the wheat from the tares and say,
*"Gather the tares in bundles and burn them in fire, but
gather the wheat into My garner"* (verse 30). This is
earth's harvesttime! This world is not going to rock on
forever the way it is now. There is coming a day of judgment when Jesus will be the Judge.

Verse 16: **"And He that sat on the cloud thrust in
His sickle on the earth; and the earth was reaped.
And another angel came out of the temple which is
in heaven, he also having a sharp sickle. And
another angel came out from the altar, which had
power over fire, and cried with a loud cry to him**

that had the sharp sickle, saying, Thrust in thy sharp sickle, and gather the clusters of the vine of the earth; for her grapes are fully ripe. And the angel thrust in his sickle into the earth, and gathered the vine of the earth, and cast it into the great winepress of the wrath of God." When Jesus comes as Judge, He will tread the winepress of the fierceness of the wrath of God Almighty! What is meant by the winepress? It is the picture of a man in a winetrough treading upon the grapes and crushing them until the juice runs out. It is a terrible figure of His judgment.

Verse 20: **"And the winepress was trodden outside the city, and blood came out of the winepress, even unto the horse bridles, by the space of a thousand and six hundred furlongs."** Two hundred miles of blood, blood, blood, blood, referring undoubtedly to the approaching Armageddon. Here the entire land of Palestine becomes a horrible winetrough with the blood of the rejectors of God and His Christ staining the land.

Beloved, we draw two things in conclusion. First, people had better come to Christ and be saved, because to be lost is horrible beyond words. Second, if we are Christians, we ought to be doing everything we possibly can to snatch souls out of the fire (Jude, verse 23).

Chapter 15

The Bowl Judgments

Verse 1. **"I saw another sign in heaven, great and marvelous, seven angels having the seven last plagues."** The word "plague" means "a blow," as when you take a stick and strike something. It means "a stroke, a wound." Here it means God's blow, God's wound, God's stroke. All through the Bible God has to do this. He doesn't want to, but people won't listen to Him any other way. He is holy. He hates sin. He must destroy it. He killed Christ for us. "It pleased the Lord to bruise Him." Somebody had to die for your sins and mine, for "the wages of sin is death." **"For in them [these blows that God sends] is filled up [completed] the wrath of God."**

Verse 2: **"And I saw as it were a sea of glass mingled with fire: and them that had gotten the victory over the beast [Antichrist], and over his image, and over his mark, and over the number of his name, stand on the sea of glass [that beautiful sea of glass before God's throne], having the harps of God. and they sang the song of Moses, the servant of God and the song of the Lamb."**

This is the victory God gave to His people, as when He brought them through the Red Sea (Exodus 15). They sang the victory song unto the Lord. The song of Moses, the servant of God, is Israel's song of deliverance by God's power, *"and the song of the Lamb"* is the song of redemption by the blood of the Lord Jesus Christ. God delivers His people by His almighty power and by the death of His Son. The blood of Christ and the power of God are for all of us who trust Christ.

"Saying, Great and marvelous are Thy works, Lord God Almighty." There is that word Almighty again, "the One who holds all things in His grasp." May I simply remind you of that, because whatever you see coming (and things will be coming), God is still sovereign, still in control! "Almighty" means "the sovereign God who holds everything in His grasp."

Let's go on: **"Just and true are Thy ways, Thou King of saints."** The better reading is, "King of the nations," as found in some of the more ancient texts. The Lord is King of the nations, Lord, Master, Ruler of all peoples. As Daniel tells us, "The Most High ruleth in the kingdom of men" (Daniel 4:32).

Then this great cry: **"Who shall not fear Thee, O Lord, and glorify Thy name? For Thou art holy: for all nations shall come and worship before Thee; for Thy judgments are made manifest."** Only by the judgments of God will nations come as nations to worship the Lord! They will not come on their own. The peoples have rejected God and His Son (Psalm 2). God's judgments must come to "bring the nations to heel." Then they will give God His proper place.

"Who shall not fear Thee, O Lord?" Somebody called me the other day and said, "Brother Jess, what is the meaning of the phrase, 'fearing the Lord'?" Through the Bible we read about fearing the Lord. For example, "The fear of the Lord is the beginning of wisdom." What does it mean to fear the Lord? Essentially, it is to live and walk with God cautiously and by faith. To do that, friends, we are careful about doing things that would hinder fellowship with God.

That is the fear of the Lord. It isn't servile fear, cringing and being afraid of God. If there is one being I have no fear of, it is God, blessed be His name! I know that He loves me! He gave His Son for me. But I am afraid to do anything that will make Him have to frown at me, or that will cause a temporary break in fellowhip with Him. This is the meaning of Paul's word, "Walk circumspectly." "On egg shells," Hendley translation. The fear of the Lord is the heart's desire to walk with God whatever the cost, and to fear anything that would hinder that walk. Now we walk by faith; hereafter we will walk by sight. I say "sight," because someday we are actually going to see the Lord! Oh, what a day that is going to be!

Verses 5,6: **"And after that I looked, and, behold, the temple of the tabernacle of the testimony in heaven was open: and the seven angels came out of the temple, having the seven plagues."** The temple down here on earth was made after the pattern of the temple in heaven. The heavenly temple is the one that abides. So these seven angels come out, **"clothed in pure white linen."** There again, I remind you that the heavenly color is white. We are going to walk with Him in white one of these days. The inheritance of the saints in light is white, the color of purity.

"And having their breasts girded with golden girdles. And one of the four living creatures gave unto the seven angels seven golden vials." The word "vial" should be "bowl." **"Full of the wrath of God."** Here again we have the wrath of God. If you have never studied the wrath of God through the Bible, I would encourage you to get your concordance and look up every reference on the wrath of God. It is mentioned eleven times in the Book of Romans alone. *"The wrath of God is revealed from heaven against all ungodliness and unrighteousness of men who hold back God's truth in unrighteousness."* Every Christian ought to master, as far as possible, Paul's epistle to the Romans.

Verse 7: **"God, who liveth unto the ages of the ages."** Here is God pouring out upon an unbelieving world His wrath. But His wrath, as I have told you, is not simply vindictive. It is designed to get people to repent, so that He can save them and bless them and bring them to glory. Those who will not repent He must put out of the way so that He can bring peace to this world. There is no other way that paradise can be regained but through the wrath of God being poured out. The wrath of God is God's removal of everything that hinders His blessing upon the rest of the race who really want to walk with Him.

Verse 8: **"And the temple was filled with smoke from the glory of God, and from His power."** That reminds us of Isaiah 6. When Isaiah was in the temple, he saw the Lord high and lifted up, and smoke filled the temple, the smoke of the shekinah glory of God. God led the people out of Egypt by a pillar of cloud by day and a pillar of fire by night. When they got up in the morning, if that cloud moved, they moved; they followed that cloud. If that column of smoke stopped, they stopped. God was guiding them, telling them when to go and when to stop. God was leading with the shekinah glory, His personal presence. Today the Father, Son, and Holy Spirit live in the believer.

Here is this temple, filled with smoke from the glory of the Lord and from His power. **"And no man was able to enter into the temple [this temple in heaven], till the seven plagues of the seven angels were fulfilled."**

This, then, is the preparation for the outpouring of the bowls of the wrath of God, seven judgments that will complete God's wrath upon an unbelieving world as He moves toward "paradise." Let me remind you again that the only way God can bring back paradise is to get rid of all people who hinder the coming of paradise, and He does that by conversion or by judgment. The Spirit of God has been in this world for some 1900 years, offering salvation and conversion to all who will believe. Most will not, so He must rid the world of the rebellious. Those who will not believe must be judged so that God can bring peace to the world.

Chapter 16

The Outpoured Bowls of God's Wrath

First Bowl

In chapter 16 we see the actual outpouring of the final bowls of God's wrath upon this unbelieving world. Verse 1: **"And I heard a great voice out of the temple saying to the seven angels, Go your ways, and pour out the bowls of the wrath of God upon the earth. And the first went, and poured out his bowl upon the earth; and there fell a noisome and grievous sore [ulcers] upon the men which had the mark of the beast, and upon them which wor-shiped his image."** We found that the Antichrist will cause his dupes to have a mark on the forehead or on the hand, and people who receive it are doomed for hell. Here is the Lord pouring out terrible ulcers that will be upon all who receive the mark of the beast.

Second Bowl

Verse 3: **"And the second angel poured out his bowl upon the sea; and it became as blood of a dead man [congealed blood in the sea]: and every living soul died in the sea."** You remember that in two of the judgments (in chapter 6 and in chapter 9) half the population of the world is destroyed. Besides that, we have these other destructions. Never in the history of this world has blood flowed as it will flow in the three and a half years before Jesus comes. It will be literally true, as the sea becomes as the putrid, horrible smell of a dead man. Jesus said that if He didn't cut this time of trouble short, no human being would be left alive on this earth. Those are His words in Matthew 24. As you read this carefully, you will find terrible destruction on every hand. Everything that lives in the sea dies. The oceans of the earth become lifeless. Nothing moves.

Third Bowl

Verse 4: **"And the third angel poured out his bowl upon the rivers and fountains of waters; and they became blood."** God is going to turn the water into blood. People won't have water to drink and will die of thirst. You can't drink blood. You can't bathe in blood. You must have water to live.

Verse 5: **"And I heard the angel of the waters say."** I pause here. We can't bring out everything in the Revelation in these messages, but I call your attention to the fact that God has special angels over certain things. One angel is over fire, another angel is over water, and another holds the winds. God has angels. People talk about "nature" and leave God completely out of the picture. Some people will not say "God." There is a studied revolt against mentioning God. They may talk about "nature," but nature is God's handiwork. The Bible says that God is operating in nature and the weather, that He makes His rain to descend upon one city and He withholds it from another (Amos 4). It is God who sends the rain. How many of us believe that He sends the rain here and stops the rain there? People are trying to run God out of His universe, but He is sovereign and He is running the show. He hasn't just wound everything up, as you wind up a clock. He doesn't let it run on its own. He is active and operative every day in the affairs of men as well as in heaven. The Lord is in control!

Verse 5: **"And I heard the angel of the waters say, Thou art righteous, O Lord, which art, and wast, and shall be, because Thou hast judged thus."** That is, You turned all the rivers and the fountains of waters into blood. You did right. **"For they have shed the blood of saints and prophets, and Thou hast given them blood to drink, for they are worthy."** Heaven says, "Amen, Lord. That's right, because they wouldn't listen to You speaking through Your messages." God's judgment on the earth will be righteous and just.

Verse 7: **"And I heard another out of the altar say, Even so, Lord God Almighty, true and righteous are Thy judgments."** Nobody will ever say, "Lord, You did wrong. You didn't do right there. You made a mistake there. Your judgment wasn't fair." Everything God does is true and right.

Fourth Bowl

Now notice the fourth bowl. Verse 8: **"And the fourth angel poured out his bowl upon the sun; and power was given unto him to scorch men with fire."** During the Tribulation Period God is going to scorch men. But have you noticed how good God is? Tonight as I was coming to church, I saw a beautiful sunset. I thought, who put that sun up there? Who keeps the earth from coming too close to it? That sun is approximately 93 million miles from the earth. If it were too far from us, we would all freeze to death; if it were too close, we would all be burned to death. Who keeps it in proper orbit?

Well, during the Tribulation Period, I don't know whether God is going to move the sun closer to the earth or move our earth closer to the sun, but men will be scorched with fire. That is a big nuclear furnace up there! Maybe God is just going to "put a little more wood on the fire." Men are going to be burned by the sun's rays. And there will be no way to escape it.

Verse 9: **"And men were scorched with great heat, and blasphemed the name of God, which hath power over these plagues."** Did men repent?

No. Rather, they blasphemed the name of God. They railed against God. They cursed God to His face. *"They repented not to give Him glory."* The main idea of these judgments is to get people to repent. If they will not repent, they will die in His judgment. To repent is to receive Christ and live to honor God.

Fifth Bowl

Notice the fifth bowl. Verse 10: **"And the fifth angel poured out his bowl upon the seat [throne] of the beast [the Antichrist]; and his kingdom was full of darkness."** I have not tried to parallel these judgments with the judgments back in Egypt in the time of Moses, but there are parallels. This one is darkness. **"And they gnawed their tongues for pain. And they blasphemed the God of heaven because of their pains and their sores, and repented not of their doings."** They repented not of the way they were living. You see, God preached His Word to us and told us how to live. But most people go on in selfishness and sin. God begins to punish. Men won't listen. He increases the punishment. Sometimes God has to do horrible things in order to get people to repent.

Sixth Bowl

Now we come to the sixth bowl in verse 12. **"And the sixth angel poured out his bowl upon the great river Euphrates [a literal river]; and the water thereof was dried up, that the way of the kings of the east might be prepared."** In the Greek it is "the way of the kings of the sunrising." Sunrising is the symbol of the Japanese. God's Word says that in the endtime there is coming a great invasion from the north: Russia is coming down into the Holy Land. There is coming an invasion from the west: the Antichrist and his ten kingdom alliance. There is coming an invasion from the east: Japan, China, India, and other nations coming across the Euphrates to invade the Holy Land in the windup. Also, the king of the south (Egypt was so called) is coming upon against Israel. All will converge on the Holy Land at the very end, just preceding Christ's return to the earth.

Verse 13: **"And I saw three unclean spirits [demons] like frogs come out of the mouth of the dragon, and out of the mouth of the wild beast [the Antichrist], and out of the mouth of the false prophet."**

Let me pause here to call your attention to the satanic trinity. The dragon is the devil; the beast is the Antichrist; the false prophet is the religious leader who will lead the worship of the Antichrist. They are imitating the Father, Son, and Holy Spirit! The devil always imitates God. The devil has always been jealous of God. He wants what God has. Read about him in Isaiah 14:14. He said, *"I will be like the Most High."* That is why he fell. He was a perfect being, one of the most beautiful that God ever made. But his heart was lifted up because of pride. He himself wanted to be God. He has challenged God ever since. And God is going to put him in his place.

Verse 14: **"For they are the spirits of devils."** Wherever you find in your King James Version the word "devils," plural, remember that it should be "demons." There is only one devil; there are many demons. The devil, Satan, is the king of the bottomless pit. These are the spirits of demons. Demons are morally and spiritually dirty in the eyes of God. **"Working miracles."** That word "miracles" is the same word used of the miracles of Jesus all through the Gospel of John. Miracles are going to return, but they will be designed to deceive people, so that they will lose their eternal souls to the devil. **"For they are the spirits of demons, working miracles, which go forth unto the kings of the earth and of the whole world, to gather them to battle of that great day of God Almighty."** Notice, they will be doing "signs," miraculous deeds that will deceive men into thinking they are from God and heaven. They will persuade all the leaders of the nations to gather their armies to Palestine where God will destroy them because they have rejected Him and His Christ. Translate the word "battle" here "war," because the word "battle" suggests the idea of one engagement. Actually, Armageddon is a series of battles, or a war.

Then the Lord says, **"Behold, I come as a thief. Blessed is he that watcheth, and keepeth his garments, lest he walk naked, and they see his shame."** Just as a thief comes unannounced, the Lord will come in sudden, unexpected judgment. This world will not be looking for these events. Myriads of people think that we are fools for studying the Word of God. To them it is a waste of time. They think more of making money and storing up treasure, of having pleasure and all the things of the earth and time. Are we wasting our time? Friends, we are the ones in the right. We can't go wrong with the Word of God! God has given us His Word. God said He will come as a thief. His judgment upon this unbelieving world will be sudden and unexpected and complete. He is almighty.

Verse 16: **"And He gathered them together into a place called in the Hebrew, Armageddon."** Some think it means "The Mount of Megiddo." A number of times it has been my pleasure to be in the north part of the land of Palestine where there is a beautiful plain. It is about 14 miles wide and 20 miles long and is called the plain of Esdraelon. The city of Megiddo, once located on the south side of the plain, is in ruins now, but it was a city that commanded the whole view of the plain. It was armed and fortified, because armies from the north and south would come through that plain ravaging little Israel. Many bloody battles mentioned in the Bible have been fought on this plain. Evidently this will be the place where the war of Armageddon will begin, at the end of the Tribulation Period.

After the Antichrist has ruled in absolute authority for three and a half years, the nations of the earth will converge on the Holy Land. God said, *"I will gather all nations against Jerusalem to battle."* In that tremendous moment in human history, God will gather all the nations and they will seek to destroy Israel. The Jews will then call on the Lord Jesus Christ. He will touch down on the Mount of Olives, and the nations will actually fight against the returning Son of God! I'll give you just one guess who is going to win.

The War of Armageddon will not only be in the north part of Palestine. Students of the Bible believe it will be more than one conflict, because in the Book of Joel, the Lord says, *"Proclaim ye this among the Gentiles: Prepare war, wake up the mighty men, let all the men of war draw near; let them come up: Beat your plowshares into swords, and your pruninghooks into spears: Let the weak say, I am strong. Assemble yourselves, and come, all ye nations. Let the nations be wakened, and come up to the valley of Jehoshaphat."* This is one of the valleys around the city of Jerusalem. *"For there will I sit to judge all the nations round about. Put ye in the sickle, for the harvest is ripe: Come, get you down; for the press is full, and the vats overflow; for their wickedness is great."* Whose wickedness? The wickedness of the nations of the earth.

"Multitudes, multitudes, in the valley of decision: for the day of the Lord is near in the valley of decision. The sun and the moon shall be darkened, and the stars shall withdraw their shining. The Lord also shall roar out of Zion, and utter His voice from Jerusalem; and the heavens and the earth shall shake [earthquake]: but the Lord will be the hope of His people, and the strength of the children of Israel."

The War of Armageddon will evidently begin in the plain of Megiddo in the north and sweep southward in and around the city of Jerusalem, and even farther south to Edom.

One of the great statements in prophecy is in Isaiah 63, concerning the returning Christ at Armageddon. Verse 1: *"Who is this that cometh from Edom with dyed garments from Bozrah? This that is glorious in His apparel, traveling in the greatness of His strength?"* This refers to Christ, and He replies, *"I who speak in righteousness, mighty to save."* Then the second question: *"Wherefore art Thou red in Thine apparel, and*

Thy garments like him that treadeth in the winefat [winepress]?" Listen to Jesus' answer: *"I have trodden the winepress alone."* He is not talking about Calvary here. This is our Lord treading out His judgment upon an unbelieving world. *"I have trodden the winepress alone; and of the people there was none with Me: for I will tread them in Mine anger."* Can you imagine Jesus saying that? *"I will trample them in My fury; and their blood shall be sprinkled upon My garments, and I will stain all My raiment. For the day of vengeance is in Mine heart, and the year of My redeemed has come."* That is exactly the picture that we have in Revelation 19, of the actual return of the Lord Jesus Christ, when His garments will be stained with the blood of His enemies.

The world doesn't know the Christ of the Bible. They think only of Jesus' love. Jesus does love us, but we'd better understand His love in the whole context of the Bible. We'd better know what the love of Jesus means. He came the first time to die for the sins of every human being. He will come the second time as Judge of everyone who does not receive Him as Savior and Lord. His judgment will be terrible, and it is coming. The Bible closes with the leaders and armies of this earth engaged in conflict against the returning Son of God.

Seventh Bowl

Verse 17: **"And the seventh angel poured out his bowl into the air; and there came a great voice out of the temple of heaven, from the throne, saying, "It is done."** "It has occurred, come into being, happened. My wrath came." These seven bowls have been poured out. God's wrath upon an unbelieving world, which He warned about in the Bible, has taken place. He did exactly what He said He would do! God keeps His promises.

Earthquakes

Verse 18: **"And there were voices and thunders and lightnings; and there was a great earthquake, such as was not since men were upon the earth; so mighty an earthquake, and so great."**

God says in Isaiah 2 that He is going to arise and *"shake terribly the earth."* Isaiah 13 says that the earth will be moved out of its orbit in the day of God's fierce anger. What will happen to this world when God picks up this globe and shakes it? People are walking around all over this earth denying His existence, hating the name of His Son, cursing His prophets, His servants, His witnesses. He is not going to put up with it forever.

Earthquakes! I read of an earthquake that rocked the southern Philippines. As many as 8,000 persons may have died from the quake and the tidal waves. Six major tremors followed the initial quake, which measured 7 on the Richter scale. Property losses were 140 million dollars, and 175,000 people were left homeless. The tidal waves touched off by the first quake were so powerful—listen—that they swept huge concrete pilings inland and hurled stingrays and sharks and other big fish on top of coconut trees. In China, there was an earthquake that measured 8.2 on the Richter scale, and 100,000 people lost their lives. There have been major earthquakes in Guatamala, in India, and in many other places in the world, devastating in their effect. The Bible says that we are coming to an earthquake period which will signal the beginning of sorrows.

In Ezekiel 38:19,20, God says (when Russia invades the Holy Land), *"In that day there shall be a great shaking in the land of Israel; so that the fish of the sea and the fowls of the heavens . . . and all the people that are upon the face of the earth shall shake at My presence, and the mountains shall be thrown down, and the steep places shall fall, and every wall shall fall to the ground."* We get our word "seismology" from the Greek word *seiein,* which means "to shake, agitate, cause to tremble."

Zechariah 14 tells us that Jerusalem will be leveled to a great plain. The Millennial temple is going to be so huge that it could not be built on the present hills about Jerusalem. When Jesus touches down on the Mount of Olives, He is going to shake that area with an earthquake. Verse 4: *"His feet shall stand in that day upon the*

Mount of Olives, which is before Jerusalem on the east, and it will cleave in the midst, and there shall be a very great valley." That hilly land will be turned into a vast level plain. Joel 3:16 says, *"The Lord shall roar out of Zion, and utter His voice from Jerusalem, and the heavens and the earth shall shake."*

Matthew 27:51 says that when Jesus was crucified God sent an earthquake that ripped the rocks, opened the graves, and some of the saints came out of their graves, walked in the holy city (Jerusalem), and appeared unto many. Their resurrection was just a little downpayment, an earnest, of the coming great first resurrection.

In Matthew 28:2, at Christ's resurrection, there was an earthquake and an angel came down and removed the stone.

Matthew 24:7 speaks of earthquakes of the endtime. Jesus, talking about the Tribulation Period, said that there shall be earthquakes in various places, and *"all these are the beginning of sorrows [woes]."* The Greek word translated "sorrows" means birthpangs. Pains increase in intensity until the birth. And after the Rapture of the church, God will begin the Tribulation Period, in the middle of which the Great Tribulation begins, when the agonies of this earth will intensify so much that nobody would be left alive if Jesus didn't come back. Then will come the birth of the new age. This age is going to die out in agony, and the new Millennial age will be born, the Kingdom of our Lord Jesus Christ.

Now together with those Scriptures, let's look again at Revelation 6:12-14. The Tribulation Period will begin with an earthquake, continue with earthquakes, and close with an earthquake that will destroy all the cities of earth, bring down every mountain to dust, and cause the islands of the sea to disappear. These verses are early in the Tribulation Period. *"When He opened the sixth seal, there was a great earthquake . . . and every mountain and island were moved out of their places."* Think of the upheaval when God shakes the entire earth!

We read of earthquakes in Revelation 8:5, 11:13, and 11:19. I have already mentioned that 7,000 people will die in the city of Jerusalem.

Then right at the end of the Tribulation, when the seventh angel pours out his bowl, there will be the greatest earthquake ever! *"And the cities of the nations fell."* New York City will be rocked to ruins in seconds and become a mass of tangled debris. So will Atlanta, and Tokyo, and Berlin. Every city on earth God is going to rock to ruins in seconds! Why? They are cesspools of iniquity in His sight. God totally destroyed Sodom and Gomorrah. The same sins are all over the earth today!

Verse 19: **"And the great city [Jerusalem] was divided into three parts, and the cities of the nations fell."** Cities, plural, the centers of population. Today more and more people are living in cities. Think of the destruction of life. I repeat, there will be a great earthquake at the beginning of the Tribulation, and earthquakes will continue, with a tremendous one at the end, closing out the wrath of God. God will level the cities of earth as Hiroshima and Nagasaki were leveled. But God's earthquakes will be far more powerful than manmade bombs! Volcanoes will be spewing everywhere. The whole earth will become a Mount St. Helens and worse. A volcano is a mountain with a lava dome and a conduit leading down to molten magma (rock) beneath. Usually an earthquake shakes the mountain open and a river of lava pours forth. I read of an island where an earthquake blew out the face of a mountain and thousands of people in the city below died in a few minutes. What will it be when God sends the most terrible earthquake in human history and every mountain and island is blown into nothingness and every city on earth destroyed? The world is "in for it," friends. That is exactly what God says. If we are wise, we will listen and believe.

Verse 20: **"And every island fled away, and the mountains were not found."** Will this make the survivors repent? Will they get on their knees and get right with God after all this destruction? Will they say,

"Lord, we've sinned against You; we know that You have brought this in order to get us to repent of sin and believe in You"? No. We'll see in a moment their reaction.

Verse 21: **"And there fell upon men a great hail out of heaven, every stone about the weight of a talent."** A talent was about 108 to 130 pounds. Can you imagine blocks of ice weighing from 108 to 130 pounds falling from the sky? That's what will happen. **"And men blasphemed God [this will be their response] because of the plague of hail; for the plague thereof was exceeding great."** No repentance, faith in the Bible, acknowledgment of God and His goodness and grace, no faith in and love for Christ who died for their sins—only continued rebellion!

Let me add this word. The longer I study the Bible, the more terrible becomes the reality of the Tribulation Period, the time of earth's greatest agony. I do not want to be here. I want to be in the Rapture with God's people who will be in heaven when the Tribulation strikes the earth. Only those who are "in Christ," dead or living, will the Lord Jesus catch up to meet Him when He comes for His bride. If you receive Jesus Christ as your Savior and trust only Him for salvation, you will be in that number.

Chapter 17

Mystery Babylon — The False World Church

"Mystery Babylon" is the apostate church of the Tribulation Period. In chapter 18 we have Babylon and its destruction. There has been uncertainty over the years among Bible students about this. Some have seen in chapters 17 and 18 the same city, Rome: in chapter 17 ecclesiastical Rome, and in chapter 18 commercial Rome. Others think they are two different cities: chapter 17 ("mystery Babylon") is Rome, the location of the false, apostate church (for the first 3 1/2 years after the Rapture) which will be destroyed by the Antichrist, and chapter 18 is the literal city of Babylon which will be rebuilt on the Euphrates River. Which of these two views is true will be revealed as world events progress toward the end of the age.

Verse 1: **"And there came out one of the seven angels which had the seven bowls, and talked with me, saying unto me, Come here, and I will show unto thee the judgment of the great harlot sitting upon many waters."** We know from verse 18 that this woman is a city: *"And the woman which thou sawest is that great city, which reigneth over the kings of the earth."*

So this harlot represents a city. "Sitting upon many waters" means ruling over the kings of the earth.

Spiritual Shame

Verse 2: **"With whom the kings of the earth have committed fornication, and the inhabitants of the earth have been made drunk with the wine of her fornication."** The Bible speaks of unfaithfulness in marriage as fornication or adultery, and these two ugly words are used of people who are unfaithful to God and His Christ. God calls Israel a harlot in Hosea 1:2 in *"departing from the Lord."* James 4:4 calls anyone who is a friend of this world an adulterer and an enemy of God! Strong words indeed. There will be a falling away before the man of sin is revealed (2 Thessalonians 2). The apostasy will develop into a great, worldwide, false church, which God calls a harlot.

False Church and Antichrist

Verse 3: **"So he carried me away in the spirit into the wilderness, and I saw a woman sit upon a scarlet-colored beast."** The woman is the false church located in Rome and the beast is the ten kingdom alliance, with the Antichrist heading it up. **"Full of names of blasphemy, having seven heads and ten horns."** We saw in preceding passages from the book of Daniel that the fourth world power is Rome, and that a coming ten kingdom alliance of nations will give the Antichrist his power.

Rome

The seven heads are definitely explained in verse 9: *"Here is the mind which has wisdom. The seven heads are seven mountains on which the woman sitteth."* So "mystery Babylon" is not literal Babylon, but Rome. The final world church will be everything God despises, because it will be a false religion deceiving the nations of earth. Notice the harlot is riding the beast. The false church will dominate Antichrist the first three and a half years after the Rapture. Then he will destroy this false church and demand that he be worshiped as God! Jesus Christ our Lord will destroy him "with the breath of His lips" and set up the Kingdom of God. Then the knowledge of the Lord shall cover the earth as the waters cover the sea.

Verse 4: **"And the woman was arrayed in purple and scarlet color, and was decked with gold and precious stones and pearls, having a golden cup in her hand full of abominations and filthiness of her fornication."** The world church will be notoriously wicked. **"And upon her forehead was a name written, MYSTERY, BABYLON THE GREAT, THE MOTHER OF HARLOTS AND ABOMINATIONS OF THE EARTH. And I saw the woman drunken with the blood of the saints, and with the blood of the martyrs of Jesus."** This false church kills a multitude of believers on Jesus (witnesses).

Verse 7: **"And the angel said unto me, Wherefore didst thou marvel? I will tell thee the mystery of the woman, and of the wild beast that carrieth her, which hath the seven heads and ten horns."** That is a clear-cut identification of the Antichrist's kingdom: the ten kingdom alliance that will furnish him with power.

Roman Empire Revived

Verse 8: **"The beast that thou sawest was, and is not; and shall ascend out of the bottomless pit, and go into perdition."** "Perdition" means "destruction," the opposite of salvation. So the Antichrist and his kingdom will arise out of the Old Roman Empire, will grow to world power, and in a short time be destroyed. These lost souls shall go into hell. **"And they that dwell on the earth shall wonder, whose names were not written in the book of life from the foundation of the world, when they behold the beast that was, and is not, and yet is."** This must be the first three and a half years of Daniel's Seventieth Week. It certainly could not take place at the close, because then the Antichrist is sitting in absolute authority, and nobody can defy him the latter three and a half years. Here is the city of Rome with a false religion in ascendancy over the Antichrist during the first half of the Tribulation Period.

Verse 9: **"Here is the mind which hath wisdom. The seven heads are seven mountains on which the woman sitteth."** The seven hills of Rome are famous in history.

Verses 10 and 11: **"And there are seven kings. Five are fallen, and one is, and the other is not yet come. And when he cometh, he must continue a short space. And the beast [Antichrist] that was, and is not, even he is the eighth [listen], and is of the seven, and goeth into perdition."** We saw in the 13th chapter that Antichrist receives a deadly wound that is healed. That means he receives a wound that kills him.

Antichrist's Resurrection

Verse 10: *"There are seven kings. Five are fallen"* *(died)*. They are dead at the time John is writing. *"One is,"* Domitian, the Emperor in John's day. *"The other is not yet come."* This refers to the future emperor who will precede the Antichrist. So out of the ten kingdom alliance an emperor will arise. He will be the seventh, and Antichrist will be the eighth. Verse 11: *"And the beast that was, and is not, even he is the eighth, and is of the seven."* This is the Antichrist, the eighth. Five emperors died. Number Six was Domitian of John's day. He was assassinated. Number Seven is not yet come; he will come at the endtime. Then the Antichrist will be Number Eight, but he is out (the Greek word is *ek*) of the seventh. How can he be the eighth, yet out of the seventh? If he is assassinated, then rises from the dead, he can be out of the seventh.

Some Bible students believe that because he is "out of the seventh" that the spirit of one of these preceding emperors will come up out of the pit and enter his body, and the Antichrist will again stand on his feet. I do not say that is so; I simply share with you the fact that it fits the language of this verse. In my years of studying the Bible, I have never found any other satisfactory explanation of this passage. The Antichrist will arise from the dead, and for this reason intelligent people all over the world will believe in him! There has been no authentic resurrection from the dead since the resurrection of Jesus. The devil is always imitating God! He has a satanic trinity and he is going to imitate the death, burial, and resurrection of the Lord Jesus Christ, and the whole world will marvel at this powerful man, the Antichrist!

Verse 12: **"And the ten horns which thou sawest are ten kings."** This is the ten kingdom alliance. **"Which have received no kingdom as yet, but receive power as kings one hour with the beast."** In Europe today, royalty doesn't have much power. England has Queen Elizabeth, but where are the European kings? John says they received no kingdom as yet, but they receive power as kings for one hour with the beast. Each king will have absolute authority and be ruler over his people. All of these kings will give their support to the Antichrist. Verse 13: **"These have one mind, and shall give their power and strength unto the beast."** This is where he gets his power!

War Against Christ

Verse 14: **"These shall make war with the Lamb."** They will together fight against Christ at the very end. The Antichrist will be there, and all the nations of the earth will be gathered together against Jerusalem, trying to exterminate the Jew when Jesus descends from heaven to the Mount of Olives. These will actually fight against the returning Jesus. They "make war with the Lamb." Friends, if I were to pick an adversary, I wouldn't pick Jesus, because the Lamb is going to win! **"The Lamb shall overcome them, for He is Lord of lords and King of kings, and they that are with Him are called, and chosen, and faithful."** I'm going to be in that crowd. If you believe in Jesus, did you know you are in the Revelation? *"They that are with Him."*

Verse 15: **"And He saith unto me, The waters**

which thou sawest, where the harlot sitteth, are peoples, and multitudes, and nations, and tongues." After the Rapture of the church, the false world church headed up in Rome will be in absolute religious authority and will rule the peoples of the world. At first, the Antichrist will be subservient to the world church, until he gains his power. Then he is going to turn against her and destroy her, as we read now: Verse 16, **"And the ten horns which thou sawest upon the beast, these shall hate the harlot and shall make her desolate and naked, and shall eat her flesh, and burn her with fire. For God hath put it in their hearts to fulfill His will and to agree and give their kingdoms unto the beast."** God is going to use the Antichrist to kill the world church. Then Christ will destroy Antichrist at His second coming!

Divine Sovereignty

"Until the words of God shall be fulfilled." I call your attention to the sovereignty of God! The Lord can control minds. God is sovereign. His will shall be done.

Daniel wrote, *"He doeth according to His will in the army of heaven, and among the inhabitants of the earth: and none can stay His hand, or say unto Him, What doest thou?"* His words shall be fulfilled! How terrible to the unbeliever! How unspeakably precious to the believing heart! God keeps His words, every one of them. Words convey thoughts. God has written His words in a book, the Bible, so that we may know His mind. *"Man,"* says Jesus, *"shall live by every word that proceeds out of the mouth of God!"* What a privilege it is to have a Bible and to study about God, the God each of us will soon meet! What a horrible error to live outside of the knowledge and fellowship of this great, living Being! Christ is the only way to know the Bible and walk with God. *"He that hath the Son hath life, and he that hath not the Son hath not life"* (I John 5:12). *"The wrath of God abideth on him"* (John 3:36). Friend, know Jesus and the Bible and you will know God, now and forever!

Chapter 18
The Fall of Babylon

As we study prophecy, we need to remind ourselves that some prophecies *have been* fulfilled, some are *being* fulfilled, and others *remain to be* fulfilled in the future. This chapter will become clear as history moves on toward the "time of the end."

There are similarities of language in chapters 17 and 18. The word Babylon is used (18:2). *The kings of the earth commit fornication with her* (17:2, 18:9). She is clothed with *gold, precious stones, and pearls* (17:4, 18:16). She is guilty of the *blood of the saints* (17:6, 18:24). She is *utterly burned with fire* (17:16, 18:8). Then in 19:1,2 *all heaven rejoices* after the destruction of the great harlot (17:1, 18:3). When I read these verses, it seems that this angel is emphasizing and adding details to the revelation of the angel of chapter 17, and that they refer to the same city.

Verses 1-3:"**And after these things I saw another angel come down from heaven, having great power, and the earth was lightened with his glory. And he cried mightily with a strong voice, saying, Babylon the great is fallen, is fallen, and is become** the habitation of devils, and the hold of every foul spirit, and a cage of every unclean and hateful bird. For all nations have drunk of the wine of the wrath of her fornication, and the kings of the earth have committed fornication with her, and the merchants of the earth are waxed rich through the abundance of her delicacies."

We have here another angel so great and powerful that he illuminated the earth coming down to announce that Babylon had fallen, because it had become a city under the control of demons and such a great commercial center that all the nations and their leaders had become infatuated with her false religion, and all the merchants of the earth had been made wealthy by her. This will evidently be the greatest business and religious city of man's history.

Verses 4-8: "And I heard another voice from heaven, saying, Come out of her, my people, that ye be not partakers of her sins, and that ye receive not of her plagues. For her sins have reached unto heaven, and God hath remembered her iniquities. Reward her even as she rewarded you, and double unto her double according to her works: in the cup which she hath filled fill to her double. How much she hath glorified herself, and lived deliciously, so much torment and sorrow give her: for she saith in her heart, I sit a queen, and am no widow, and shall see no sorrow. Therefore shall her plagues come in one day, death, and mourning, and famine; and she shall be utterly burned with fire: for strong is the Lord God who judgeth her."

Another voice from heaven calls the godly people to leave immediately because her sins have piled up to heaven, and the danger of yielding to her sinful temptations is so great that if they stay, they will be punished by God along with her. He has remembered her iniquities and she shall receive double torment, though she boasts she shall never pay for her evil. In one day God will destroy her with death, mourning, and famine, and she will be destroyed by fire. The Lord God who judgeth her is strong enough to destroy her and the entire universe (II Peter 3:10).

Verses 9-19: "**And the kings of the earth, who have committed fornication and lived deliciously with her, shall bewail her, and lament for her, when they shall see the smoke of her burning, Standing afar off for the fear of her torment, saying, Alas, alas, that great city Babylon, that mighty city! for in one hour is thy judgment come.**

"**And the merchants of the earth shall weep and mourn over her; for no man buyeth their merchandise any more: The merchandise of gold, and silver, and precious stones, and of pearls, and fine linen, and purple, and silk, and scarlet, and all thyine wood, and all manner vessels of ivory, and all manner vessels of most precious wood, and of brass, and iron, and marble, and cinnamon, and odours, and ointments, and frankincense, and wine, and oil, and fine flour, and wheat, and beasts, and sheep, and horses, and chariots, and slaves, and souls of men. And the fruits that thy soul lusteth after are departed from thee, and all things which were dainty and goodly are departed from thee, and thou shalt find them no more at all.**

"**The merchants of these things which were made rich by her, shall stand afar off for the fear of her torment, weeping and wailing, and saying, Alas, alas that great city, that was clothed in fine linen, and purple, and scarlet, and decked with gold, and precious stones, and pearls! For in one hour so great riches is come to nought.**

"**And every shipmaster, and all the company in ships, and sailors, and as many as trade by sea, stood afar off, and cried when they saw the smoke of her burning, saying, What city is like unto this great city! And they cast dust on their heads, and cried, weeping and wailing, saying, Alas, alas that great city, wherein were made rich all that had ships in the sea by reason of her costliness! for in one hour is she made desolate.**" The kings and the merchants of earth wail over her destruction for "no man buyeth their merchandise any more" (v. 11), and "in one hour so great riches is come to nought" (v. 17).

Verses 20-24: **"Rejoice over her, thou heaven, and ye holy apostles and prophets; for God hath avenged you on her. And a mighty angel took up a stone like a great millstone, and cast it into the sea, saying, Thus with violence shall that great city Babylon be thrown down, and shall be found no more at all.**

"And the voice of harpers, and musicians, and of pipers, and trumpeters, shall be heard no more at all in thee; and no craftsman, of whatsoever craft he be, shall be found any more in thee; and the sound of a millstone shall be heard no more at all in thee;

"And the light of a candle shall shine no more at all in thee; and the bride of the bridegroom and of the bride shall be heard no more at all in thee: for thy merchants were the great men of the earth; for by thy sorceries were all nations deceived. And in her was found the blood of prophets, and of saints, and of all that were slain upon the earth."

Heaven and the godly apostles and prophets are told to rejoice over her doom, for God has avenged her. She has resisted God's witnesses and the Bible, and now God avenges them. She is violently thrown down and totally destroyed. No more music, no more craft, not even a candle shines in their homes at night. No more wedding ceremonies. The great men of earth are shocked at her ruin. They realize they were deceived, tricked, by her sorceries.

Verse 24: God holds her responsible for the blood of the prophets and of the saints and of all the godly that were killed on earth! So this is a great anti-God city. In this chapter we have clear statements that demons are here on earth and sophisticated people will be persuaded to follow their teaching. The devil and his demons will deceive the world. People will reject Christ and follow them.

In Genesis 11:1-9 we read of the great anti-God movement at Babel, and how God judged the rebellious nations by confounding their language and scattering men over the face of the earth.

Bible prophecy here in the Revelation leaps across the centuries and shows us the human race in rebellion which God will wipe out forever! Those who will not have God as Saviour must take Him as Judge.

Babylon! A wicked, commercial city where everybody is interested in one thing: making money! Are we not headed for that now? Oh, what a message could be brought on "The Sin of Covetousness." God equates covetousness with idolatry. Children these days are raised to believe that the first thing in life is having money; do anything else you want to do, but just make the money. Give your life to making money. Covetousness is the inordinate desire to have more and more, without considering the will of God. People all over the world are selling their very souls because of the sin of covetousness. Several businessmen have said to me, "You can't put Christian principles to work out there in the business world." That isn't true. Although it is difficult, it can be done. Many Christian businessmen are indeed putting Christian principles to work. It is interesting to notice the last line of the book of Zechariah: "There shall be no more Canaanite in the house of the Lord of hosts." That Hebrew word "Canaanite" means "trafficker." The man who is just "out to make it" is trafficking. God is going to change this world system someday!

God says, *"See first the Kingdom of God and His right-* **eousness and all things shall be added unto you"** (Matthew 6:33). "Cast all your care upon Him for He careth for you" (I Peter 5:7). How wonderful to have God supplying all our need "according to His riches in glory by Christ Jesus" (Philippians 4:19).

Notice the repetition in verses 17 and 19 that "in one hour's time" the city is made desolate. *A mighty angel took up a stone like a great millstone, and cast it into the sea, saying, Thus with violence shall that great city Baby-*

lon be thrown down, and shall be found no more at all."
The city is completely destroyed.

There are men who believe that Babylon will be rebuilt. I was interested to read in a well-known national magazine that Iran has plans to rebuild Babylon. They have oil. Already they have put on a display of ancient Babylon and are talking about rebuilding it. Some say Babylon was never totally destroyed, as spoken of by Isaiah and Jeremiah, that the Arabians still pitch their tents there, and therefore this destruction of Babylon (in chapter 18 of the Revelation) comes at the very endtime, just before Jesus returns. Time will tell.

Chapter 19

The Marriage of the Lamb

Heaven Rejoicing

"And after these things I heard a great voice of much people in heaven saying, Alleluia: salvation, and glory, and honor, and power, unto the Lord our God: for true and righteous are His judgments. For He hath judged the great harlot which did corrupt the earth with her fornication and hath avenged the blood of His servants at her hand." (vv. 1,2). This is the first of four Hallelujahs in heaven. *Hallelu* is "praise ye," and *jah* is the abbreviation of God's personal name, Yahweh. Here are the people in heaven rejoicing over the destruction of Mystery Babylon, the false church. You say, "Is that Christlike?" Yes. It is both Christlike and Godlike. Christ is God, of course. God absolutely must destroy that which is false, and He is going to do it.

Verse 3: "**And again they said, Alleluia. And her smoke rose up unto the ages of the ages. And the four and twenty elders and the four living creatures fell down and worshiped God that sat on the throne, saying, Amen; Alleluia. And a voice came out of the throne, saying, Praise our God, all ye His** servants, and ye that fear Him, both small and great. And I heard as it were the voice of a great multitude, and as the voice of many waters, and as the voice of mighty thunderings, saying, Alleluia: for the Lord God omnipotent reigneth." God is ruling this world this very hour! He is pulling the strings. He is moving in the background, toward the time when He takes over the direct rule of this world. In heaven they praise God for salvation, for His righteous judgments, for His sovereignty. What a day it is going to be when God takes over the government of this world! It is written in Isaiah 9 concerning Christ, *"The government shall be upon His shoulder, and His name shall be called Wonderful, Counselor, The Mighty God, The Everlasting Father, The Prince of Peace."* How wonderful our Lord Jesus Christ will be! In verse 6, the volume of praise is so great that it reminds John of a mighty waterfall and repeated thunderings.

The Marriage of the Lamb

In verses 7 and 8 we come to the marriage supper, or the Marriage of the Lamb. **"Let us be glad and rejoice, and give honor to Him, for the marriage of the Lamb has come, and His wife hath made herself ready. And to her was granted that she should be arrayed in fine linen, clean and white. For the fine linen is the righteousness of the saints."**

The marriage of the Lamb! This passage deserves a full message, beloved, when Jesus takes His bride unto Himself in glory. This takes place before we come back with Him to the Mount of Olives. He is going to present the church to Himself *"a glorious church, not having spot, nor wrinkle, nor any such thing, but that she should be holy and without blemish"* (Ephesians 5:27). What a day it is going to be when Jesus takes us to Himself!

The very first marriage was in the Garden of Eden when God created the woman and brought her to the man. He said, *"It is not good for man to be alone. I will make him a helpmeet."* God Himself performed the first wedding ceremony. That must have been some wedding. She must have been some bride! He must have been some bridegroom! Perfect! Can you imagine a perfect man and a perfect woman in a perfect environment? No bad nature, no wrong thoughts, no wrong words, no wrong deeds. Perfect! Paradise! Wow!

We read in the Bible about Abraham and his Sarah, about Isaac and his Rebekah, about Jacob who served 14 years to win Rachel. Christ left heaven and died to win us! In the beautiful 24th chapter of Genesis, the elder servant was sent by Abraham to go and find a bride for Isaac. It is a picture of the Holy Spirit going out and finding the bride for Christ, gathering us unto the Lord. Can you imagine what it is going to be like when suddenly our Lord descends from heaven with the shout of a bridegroom? Who ever heard of a bridegroom who didn't want his bride? Or of a bride who didn't want her bridegroom? Jesus certainly wants us, and we ought to want Him. At the close of the Revelation He says, *"Behold, I am coming quickly."* And John represents the church in saying, *"Amen, Lord. Come quickly!"* That is the response of the bride.

Also in the Old Testament we read that Israel is called the wife of Jehovah, the wife of the Lord. The book of Hosea depicts God's love for Israel. If you want to study the love of God, dig into the book of Hosea. God loved that nation that deserted Him as a husband grieves over his departed wife. Hosea has always been one of my favorites. His language is out of this world! Through Hosea, God said to Israel, *"I love you. As a bridegroom rejoiceth over his bride, so shall I God rejoice over thee."* That is how much God loved Israel, and still does. How much does the Lord Jesus love us this very moment? As a bridegroom rejoiceth over his bride!

One day my wife and I took a little boat trip from Miami to Bimini. We saw lots of interesting things. Flying fish. Have you ever seen flying fish? They jump up out of the water because something is trying to gobble them down. So they fly up and out. We saw the captain of the boat land a big sailfish and throw it back into the water. We saw the beauty of the water and the little island of Bimini with its gorgeous tropical flowers and palm trees. But there was a young couple on board who didn't see any of that. They had just been married, and all that young man saw was that girl. And all that girl saw was that young man. All they saw was each other! They didn't see any flying fish or beautiful water and gorgeous flowers and palm trees.

May I use that as a parable? Beloved, when we get up there and see JESUS, we might see the golden streets or the pearly gates—after a billion years—and we might glance around at all the glories of heaven, but our heart's love and attention will be upon HIM. If the love of our Christ that we enjoy down here now is so overwhelming, what will it be when we are actually in His presence? Christ as the Bridegroom will reach out and take His bride into His arms! I am not stretching language. *"The marriage of the Lamb has come. His wife has made herself ready."* The Bride and the Bridegroom will be together at last—forever! How precious to know that by faith I am a member of the Bride of Christ.

Then Christ through John tells us the bridal attire. Her clothing will be of the finest linen, brilliant to the sight and spotlessly new. How could it be otherwise when the garments are His gift to her? Oh, beloved, this is the fruit of His death on the cross where *"by one offering He perfected us forever."* This is the fulfillment of the Spirit's words to Paul: *"Christ loved the church, and gave Himself for it, that He might sanctify and cleanse it, that He might present it to Himself a glorious church, not having spot, or wrinkle, but that it should be holy and without blemish"* (Ephesians 5:25-27). And again in Romans 8:30, *"Whom He justified, them He also glorified."* We are not yet in glory, but it is as good as done because God says so. We are already glorified in God's unfailing purpose, and we shall owe it all to JESUS forever!

The Bridal Dress

John explains that the fine linen represents the "righteous acts of the saints." Saints are people who are justified, declared right by God, when they trust

JESUS. Then they read the Bible and do the will of God. These doings of saved people are called by Paul in Ephesians 2:10 *"good works, which God hath before ordained that we should walk therein."* We do no work to be saved. Jesus saved us by His work for us on the cross. But saved people work out of love for Him.

Here we have *all* the good works of *all* God's people, which will be the bridal dress in which we shall meet the Bridegroom. He will honor every one of us for all we have done for Him in our lives, even though *"it is God who works in us both the willing and the doing of His good pleasure"* (Philippians 2:13). What a day that will be! If we really believe these words we will be trusting JESUS alone for salvation, and we will realize that the most important thing in our lives will be the doing of righteous acts He has for us to do. "To every man his work." Of a blessed woman Jesus said, "She has done what she could." God help us to be busy about the work of the Lord.

The Marriage Supper

Verse 9: **"Write, Blessed are they which are called unto the marriage supper of the Lamb. And he saith unto me, These are the true sayings of God. And I fell at his feet to worship him. And he said unto me, See thou do it not, for I am thy fellow servant, and of thy brethren that have the testimony of Jesus. Worship God. For the testimony of Jesus is the spirit of prophecy."** Who is this who commands John to write? He describes himself in verse 10 as a "fellow-slave," "a brother" in the same family of God with John and one who "keeps holding" Jesus' testimony. (Heaven believes in the Deity and words of Jesus.) This evidently is an angel, for we have similar words in Revelation 22:8,9. John, because the voice came out of the Throne of God, prostrated himself in an attitude of reverence. The angel quickly corrected him: "See thou do it not," meaning, "Don't worship me; worship God." In Luke 20:36, Jesus says that in the resurrection we shall be "equal to the angels."

What did he tell John to write? That people who accepted God's invitation to the marriage supper of the Lamb are the truly "blessed," the happiest people who ever lived. In Matthew 5:3-11 this word is used nine times. A life of true happiness is lived only by those who believe in Jesus Christ for salvation and seek to live pleasing to Him by the power of the Holy Spirit. Since the church is the Bride of Christ, these "invited" ones must be the saved of times other than the church age, which is from Pentecost to the Rapture: the saved of the Old Testament and the Tribulation Period. Notice that what Jesus said is in accord with all that the prophets of God spoke. They *"spoke from God, being carried along by the Holy Spirit"* (II Peter 1:21). Men had better heed the words of this book; for the testimony of Jesus is the Word of God (Revelation 1:2).

Christ's Second Coming

Verse 11: **"And I saw heaven opened, and behold, a white horse, and He that sat upon it was called Faithful and True."** *The Fifth Horseman!*

John tells us 55 times what he saw in the spirit. The prophets of Old Testament times were called seers. Seers! They saw things by the Spirit what man could never see naturally! John saw farther into eternity and deeper into the mind and heart of God than others. "Heaven opened." There are three heavens. This is the third, as Paul tells us. In Revelation 4:1 John saw a door opened in heaven, and a voice summoned him, "Come up here." All heaven is opened to reveal the glorified Christ as He prepares to descend to the Mount of Olives on earth.

"And behold a white horse." White is the color of heaven, the color of purity. There is nothing impure there.

His Character

"And He that sat upon him was called Faithful and True." He is Faithful, meaning trustworthy, reliable, sure. If you trust your soul and your eternity to anyone but Jesus, you are to be pitied. He is True, meaning real, ideal, genuine. You can count on His work for you

on the cross where He put away your sins. You can count on His promises to you in the Bible. The rider on the white horse in 6:2 is the Antichrist, a deceiver, an imitator of Christ. He destroys. Jesus saves! Praise Him. Trust Him only. There is no other trustworthy. Paul was persuaded that Christ would "keep my deposit" (II Timothy 1:12). He had placed his most precious treasure, his eternal soul, into Christ's hands for safekeeping. So have I. Have you?

"And in righteousness he doth judge and make war." Christ judging people? Christ making war with people? Yes! *"The Father hath committed all judgment unto the Son"* (John 5:22). Is this the meek and lowly Jesus of the gospels who died for the world's sins, arose from the dead, and says, *"Come unto Me, all ye that labor and are heavy laden, and I will give you rest"?* Yes, He is the same. He never changes. But we must remember God gave a twofold work to Him to do. He sent Him the first time to suffer and die to provide salvation for all of us. This He did, and we are living in the age of grace when God forgives everyone who trusts Jesus. But most people will not receive Him and they must be removed before there can be peace on earth. So God will send Him back as Judge. Nobody will spit on Him, beat Him, mock Him, crucify Him. His sufferings will then be over forever.

His Appearance

Verses 12 and 13:**"His eyes were as a flame of fire, and on his head were many crowns; and he had a name written, that no man knew, but he himself. And he was clothed with a vesture dipped in blood: and his name is called the Word of God."** At His first coming He was in a human body, subject to sickness, pain and death, and unattractive to natural eyes. Isaiah said, *"He was despised and rejected of men, a man of sorrows and acquainted with grief,"* and *"He hath no form nor comeliness and when we shall see Him there is no beauty that we should desire Him."* Christ's second coming will be totally different. John here describes His eyes. Once filled with sorrow, now they are full of fiery indignation against rebellious man. His head, once bowed in shame as He became sin for us, now is crowned with many kingly diadems! All rulers on earth will disappear and the authority over all nations will be His alone!

His Name

His Name. He was called Jesus Savior, by the angel of the Lord at His first coming (Matthew 1:21). Now He has a private, personal name, given by the loving Father to the Son in whom He delights, the Son who obeyed Him always, even to the death of the cross. It is a name He alone knows, a name reserved for the loving intimacy of the three members of the Godhead, the Father, the Son, and the Holy Spirit. What human being can ever fathom the depths of the love of one Divine Being for another? We have the high privilege of sharing that love, but we'll be learning more and more throughout the ages to come, of the exceeding riches of His grace in His kindness toward us through Christ Jesus, His Beloved Son! (Ephesians 2:7).

His Clothing

His clothing, His outer garment, mantle, cloak, is sprinkled with the blood of His enemies. In Isaiah 63:3,4 Christ foretells His coming as a mighty conqueror: *"I will tread [the people] in mine anger and trample them in my fury; and their blood shall be sprinkled upon my garments, and I will stain all my raiment."* Those who say, "We will not have this man reign over us," must go. He Himself says, *"He that is not with Me is against Me!"* Everyone must receive Jesus as Saviour or meet Him as Judge. Why? Because God's purpose is to bring peace to the world. The only way to have peace is to get rid of non-peaceful people. The only way to do this is by conversion or judgment. For nearly 2000 years God has offered mankind His Son as Savior. There are more unbelievers today than when Christ came. More people were born today than will receive Christ. The world is becoming more pagan every day.

God, in order to bring peace, is left with nothing but judgment. So God is moving through judgment to a world of peace. We who believe look for a new heaven and a new earth wherein dwells righteousness (people and things that are right in God's eyes).

How many people know this Christ? Know that He is Savior but also Judge? That He is loving but also holy? He is Lamb but also Lion? Merciful but also righteous? That He saves those who believe, but to those who refuse Him as Savior and Lord He becomes a Consuming Fire?

Christ, the Word of God

He will be recognized by all as the Word of God. Words convey thought. "The Word" is the total message of God. God wanted us to know His mind, His pity, His love for us, His saving grace. He sent His prophets and apostles with the spoken and written Word. He sent His Son as His Living Message to us, sent Him not only to speak His thoughts, but to live them before us. The greatest message Christ brought us is the Word of the cross, where God spelled out His total love for every human being.

We read of Christ the Word of God in John 1:1. He existed before the beginning of time, co-equal with God, in communication with God. He became a human being to bring us God's message. In 1 John 1:1 again He is the Word sent to bring us eternal life and fellowship with Himself and the Father. Here in Revelation He is the great Consummator. He will fulfill God's plan to destroy the present heavens and earth and bring in a new heaven and new earth and endless peace (Isaiah 9:6,7).

Verse 14: **"And the armies which were in heaven followed Him upon white horses, clothed in fine linen, white and clean."** Who will these be? Certainly all the holy angels, and there are more than one hundred million of these super-earthly beings. Also all the saved of the church age who will have been caught up at the Rapture, taken to heaven (John 14:1-3), rewarded at the Judgment Seat of Christ, and who have participated in the Marriage of the Lamb. For it is written, *"So shall we ever be with the Lord,"* after the Rapture. We, together with all the angels of God, shall line the highway from heaven to earth to attend Christ as He comes again. Every true believer! Once with Christ, we shall never leave Him, nor He us.

Notice that the armies don't do the fighting. Verse 15: **"Out of His mouth goeth a sharp sword, that with it He should smite the nations."** He is the one who will put down the enemies. **"And He shall rule them with a rod of iron [in the Millennium]: and He treadeth the winepress of the fierceness and wrath of Almighty God."** The sharp sword that John sees going out of His mouth is His Word. Isaiah 11:4, *"With the breath of His lips shall He slay the wicked."* He, Himself the Word, needs only to speak a word, and it will be done. He is God. With a deadly blow He will strike the nations (which means Gentiles, as distinct from Israel). He will rule them with an iron rod in the Millennium and He Himself will tread the winetrough. This is the breaking out of the fiery heat of the deep anger which God Almighty possesses! That is why the blood is sprinkled on His garments. It is the picture of a man who owns a vineyard. He gathers the grapes, casts them into the winepress, takes off His shoes, steps in, and crushes the grapes beneath his feet. The juice spatters up on his garments. It is the picture of Christ coming in judgment upon this unbelieving world.

Verse 16: **"And He hath on His vesture and on His thigh a name written, KING OF KINGS, AND LORD OF LORDS."** King of kings and Lord of lords! *King of kings and Lord of lords!* KING OF KINGS AND LORD OF LORDS! Our Jesus, this One to whom we have entrusted our souls, is King of kings and Lord of lords! Amen! God will give THE WORLD to His Son!

Remember these things about God and His Son:

1. God loves His Son as no earthly father could ever love his son (Proverbs 8:22-30).
2. The world has largely rejected God and His Son (Psalm 2).

3. God's plan for His Son is world dominion
   (Isaiah 9:6,7).
4. God will give this world to His Son at the Second
   Coming (Daniel 7:9,10,13,14).
5. Christ will return to take the world by force
   (Revelation 19:11-16).

The study of the Scriptures reveals why God will have these words, King of Kings and Lord of Lords, inscribed on the garment and thigh of His Son when He returns. Christ is the KING, who rules all other kings and to whom all other kings are subject. Christ is the supreme master over all other masters. It is right for God to do this for Him, because Christ was ever and always the perfect Son, *"obedient unto death, even the death of the cross. Wherefore* [because God told Him to offer His life as a substitute for us lost sinners and He obeyed Him] *God hath highly exalted Him and given Him a name which is above every name, that at the name of JESUS every knee should bow* [in prostration, adoration, subjection], *and that every tongue should confess that Jesus Christ is Lord."* (Philippians 2:9-11). MASTER! Oh, this Wonderful Person! What a privilege God has given us to believe in Him and know Him and walk with Him and fellowship with Him and His Father forever!

Feast for Birds

Verses 17 and 18: **"And I saw an angel standing in the sun; and he cried with a loud voice, saying to all the fowls that fly in the midst of heaven, Come and gather yourselves together unto the supper of the great God; that you may eat the flesh of kings, and the flesh of captains, and the flesh of mighty men, and the flesh of horses, and of them that sit on them, and the flesh of all men, both free and bond, both small and great."**

Here we have God commanding a horrible feast for the birds. A mighty angel is seen standing in the sun (heat can do no harm to a heavenly being, Daniel 3:25). He cries to all the birds to assemble to the greatest feast God ever prepared for them (He feeds the birds,

Matthew 6:26). Their food will be the bodies of kings and captains and all who have rejected Him and His Son.

This is the actual Battle of Armageddon, involving the beast (Antichrist) and his ten-kingdom alliance; the king of the north (Syria in Old Testament days); Russia with her allies from the uttermost parts of the north (Ezekiel 38:6,15); the king of the south (which was Egypt in Old Testament days), undoubtedly with her allies (Daniel 11:40); the kings of the east (Revelation 16:12, 13:9-16). The military from all nations (Zechariah 14:1) will assemble in the Holy Land where they literally will try to fight against the returning Almighty Son of God. Earthly armies versus the heavenly!

Our Lord Himself destroys the armies of earth. This is the end of all war. This is the end of all armies. After Armageddon, no more Annapolis, no more West Point. The Psalmist said, *"He will make war to cease to the ends of the earth"* (46:9).

"And the beast was taken, and with him the false prophet that wrought the miracles before him, with which he deceived them that received the mark of the beast, and them that worshiped his image. These both were cast alive into the lake of fire burning with brimstone. And the remnant were slain with the sword of Him that sat upon the horse, which sword proceeded out of His mouth: and all the fowls were filled with their flesh." The Antichrist and the false prophet will be captured by Christ and His armies. Living, they will be thrown into the lake of fire burning with brimstone, which is the final hell. They are the first two occupants and are alive there after the 1,000-year reign of Christ on earth (Revelation 20:10). The devil and all the unsaved will be thrown into this place of horrors (Revelation 20:15). This is what "shall not perish" means in John 3:16, God's precious promise to believers.

Chapter 20

God's Plan for the Future

We come now to the final three chapters of the book. Remember that God has a vast overall plan. The Bible didn't "grip" me until I found that God is moving in history according to a specific plan.

In the book of Genesis we read about God creating Adam and Eve and putting them in paradise, a perfect environment. Adam and Eve had the liberty of obeying God or Satan, and they chose Satan. Eve was deceived, but Adam was not deceived. He knew what he was doing when he sinned against God. As a consequence, the entire human family who descended from him has been born with a sinful nature. But we have the choice of whether we want to come out of it and move into God's fellowship and blessing and paradise. There is a way out, through Christ!

In order to offer paradise to us, God gave to His Son Jesus the task of redemption. It was twofold: He was to come the first time as Savior, and the second time as Judge. He came to die on the cross, to provide salvation for all of Adam's race, sinners who were born in sin and who chose to sin. He shed His blood to atone for all sin,

that whosoever believes in Him shall not perish but
have everlasting life. The cross of Jesus was the place
where your salvation and mine was accomplished.

But God said that Christ would come the second time
to complete the plan of redemption. He will completely
destroy everything that has the vestige or stain of sin
upon it. Even the heavens were stained with sin when
the devil rebelled against God and fell. So the heavens
will be replaced. God is going to destroy the present
heavens and earth, and there will be new heavens and
new earth wherein dwells nothing but righteousness.
So far as I know, the only mark of sin that will be in the
new creation will be the blessed scars of the Lord Jesus,
reminding us of His crucifixion for us.

So our Lord Jesus was given the responsibility of
bringing paradise back to this earth. But for people
who refuse to be converted, there is nothing left but
judgment. God has no alternative. Only through judgment can paradise be restored, and that is what God is
doing. That is how the love of God and the wrath of God
are brought together. They are both true. God is love;
He forgives and saves sinners. But God is also righteous
and just; His wrath will come upon all who will (in His
words) "destroy the earth."

Our Lord is coming again, and this Book of the Revelation tells about the consummation of the ages. We
read how Jesus took the little book out of the Father's
hand and tore open the seals. We studied about the Seal
Judgments, the Trumpet Judgments, and the Bowl
Judgments. Now we come to the conclusion of it all as
God creates a new, perfect paradise for born-again men
and women who have chosen Him. Just as Adam chose
between God and Satan, so also men and women down
through the centuries have chosen between God and
Satan. Those who have chosen God and holiness will
eventually be in the Holy City.

Satan Bound During Millennium

Let's turn now to Revelation 20. Before there can be
the promised paradise, the devil must be removed from

the scene. Christ and the devil cannot rule at the same time. The evil one, the deceiver, the destroyer, cannot rule at the same time with the Holy One, the Truth, the Savior! Three times Jesus said that the devil is "the ruler of this world" and that He and the devil have absolutely nothing in common. "The world" means all the ungodly, who reject Christ as Savior. Paul tells us that Satan is *"the spirit who is continually working in people who are disobedient to God"* (Ephesians 2:2). John tells us that *"the whole world lieth in the power [helpless, in the grip] of the devil"* (I John 5:19). This explains why people do horrible things. They are in the power of the devil. All persons who are not in Christ (and this includes so-called "good people" who refuse Christ) are in the power of the evil one, and ultimately, because they have rejected Christ, they will be lost.

In this chapter the devil is bound. **"And I saw an angel come down from heaven, having the key of the bottomless pit and a great chain in his hand. And he laid hold on the dragon, that old serpent, which is the Devil and Satan, and bound him a thousand years, and cast him into the bottomless pit, and shut him up, and set a seal upon him, that he should deceive the nations no more, till the thousand years should be fulfilled; and after that he must be loosed a little season."**

For a thousand years there will be no devil tempting men anywhere on the face of the earth. Here is a strong angel capable of binding the devil by the power God gives to him. This angel descends into the air (Satan is "prince of the power of the air") with the key that will unlock the door at the top of the shaft leading down into the boundless place called "the abyss" (Revelation 9:1,2), where demons are imprisoned, and from which the Antichrist will ascend (Revelation 11:7), and where the destroyer, the devil, is king. This angel has a massive chain. He immobilizes the devil, the most deadly being in the universe — the dragon, the monster, the original serpent that tempted Adam and Eve, the slanderer who falsely accuses us before God day and night, and our adversary, our enemy! The angel binds him and throws him down the shaft into the pit. He shuts and locks the door. He seals it, making certain that the deceiver of the nations cannot cause them to turn from God until the thousand years of Christ's reign on earth are fulfilled.

Then it is necessary for Satan to be set free again for a short time. Why? Because in every generation God has allowed Satan to test men. The test is whether we believe God's Word or the devil's. The people born during the Millennium will not have been tested as to their faith, so God will allow Satan to be set free from the pit and roam the earth just as he does today. The devil, *"as a roaring lion, walketh about, seeking whom he may devour"* (I Peter 5:8). We must make our choice, whether the Lord Jesus Christ or the devil rules our lives. Jesus said to certain people of His day, *"Ye are of your father, the devil"* (John 8:44). He also said that before His return the devil would deceive, if possible, the very elect (Matthew 24:24). Why do people perish? Because *"They receive not the love of the truth, that they might be saved"* (II Thessalonians 2:10).

Christ's Millennial Kingdom

We have the beginning of the Millennium in verse 4. **"And I saw thrones, and they that sat upon them, and judgment was given unto them. And I saw the souls of them that were beheaded for the witness of Jesus, and for the Word of God, and which had not worshiped the beast [the Antichrist], neither his image, neither had received his mark upon their foreheads, or in their hands; and they lived and reigned with Christ a thousand years."** The Millennium! You will find the thousand years mentioned six times in the Revelation. All through the Bible the thousand-year reign of Christ is foretold. It is in the prophetic writings. It is in Jesus' teachings. All through the Word we read of the coming "Kingdom of God," when the kingdom of this world shall become the kingdom of our Lord and of His Christ and He shall reign forever and ever.

Thrones

Verse 4. **"And I saw thrones, and they that sat on them."** "They" refers to the church, because again and again we find the twenty-four elders round about the throne, representing the church of the Lord Jesus Christ. They are said to reign with Him. Also, in Revelation 2:26 and 3:21, Jesus said He would grant to the overcomer to sit with Him on His throne, even as He overcame and sat down with His Father on His throne. So the church will be elevated to sit with Christ and reign with Him over this entire earth for a thousand glorious years. The people saved during the Tribulation, Jews and Gentiles, will be in their natural bodies, and we Christians will be in our glorified bodies on thrones with the Lord Jesus, reigning over them.

Christ will literally reign from the literal, enlarged city of Jerusalem (Zechariah 14:9-11). He will rebuild the temple, called the Millennial Temple of Christ. It is detailed for us in Ezekiel 40-48. The capital city of the world will be Jerusalem—not Washington or Tokyo or Berlin or any of these others. Jerusalem will be the Holy City, and Christ will reign over the entire earth from the temple that He will rebuild.

Under Him will be the twelve apostles, who will be over the twelve tribes of Israel. David will be over the entire kingdom of Israel. In the 37th chapter of Ezekiel, David is called king and prince on two different occasions. There is another reference to him in Hosea. So David, resurrected from the dead, will be given rulership over the nation of Israel under Christ during the Millennium.

Believers will be ruling over the other nations of earth. You remember what Jesus taught in one of His parables: *"Have thou authority over ten cities. Have thou authority over five cities."* I pause to remind us that our place in the Millennium is being determined now, in this life, according to our works. God's Word teaches that. Our work for Christ here determines our position in the Millennium! We get into it by God's grace. We are born into the kingdom by the second birth, the spiri-

tual birth Jesus taught Nicodemus in John 3. He said
that a man cannot enter the kingdom unless he is born
again. The entrance is right now, in this life, by believing in Jesus as our Savior and Lord. When we are born
again, we are assured of a place in the Millennium. But
our position will be determined by our works.

These believers on the thrones were given elevated
positions of judging. Paul wrote to the Corinthians,
*"Know ye not that the saints shall judge the world? We
shall judge angels."* Can you imagine that? There we
will be — just sinners who should have been condemned
for our sins, but saved by the amazing grace of God!
Saved forever, when we believed on Jesus! Someday we
shall reign with Him. Being His bride, of course we
shall ever be with the Lord. What a marvelous future
awaits the children of God!

Tremendous World Changes

We read in the book of Isaiah about tremendous
world changes that will take place under Christ's
blessed rule. War will be banished (2:4). Righteousness
will prevail (11:4). The ferocity of wild beasts will be removed (11:6-8). There will be no violence and harm, because the knowledge of the Lord will cover the earth
(11:9). Sickness will be diminished (33:24). Deserts
will be reclaimed to take care of an unparalleled population explosion (35:1). Israel will be the leading
nation (ch. 60), as God fulfills His promise to the
nation He loves with undying love (Jeremiah 31:3). A
remnant, a fraction, will be delivered (Zechariah
14:11-21) from her enemies and regathered (Isaiah
60:9) from the nations to her land. God will enter into
an unconditional covenant with her, unlike the Sinai
Covenant. The temple will be rebuilt by Christ (Ezekiel
40-48, Zechariah 6:12,13). Jerusalem will be called
"The Lord is there" (Ezekiel 48:35).

Glorified Bodies

Christians will be in their glorified bodies
(Philippians 3:21) given to them at the Rapture. The

body will be like Christ's resurrection body that walked through locked doors in the upper room, appeared and disappeared as when He walked on the Emmaus road (Luke 24), a body spiritually fit for heaven and earth, which Thomas touched (John 20:26). We will be with Christ and like Christ (I John 3:2) and have authority over cities of earth (Luke 19:17,19). This world will become peaceful at last under the beneficent rule of Christ and His saints.

To enter the Kingdom, we must be born from above (John 3:5-7), for only the life of God can go to God. People who have faith in Christ will feast with Abraham, Isaac, and Jacob in the kingdom (Matthew 8:11,12).

The Second Resurrection

Verse 5: **"But the rest of the dead lived not again until the thousand years were finished. This is the first resurrection. Blessed and holy is he that hath part in the first resurrection. On such the second death hath no power, but they shall be priests of God and of Christ, and shall reign with Him a thousand years."** This is the only identification in the Bible, so far as I know, of the time-lapse between the two great resurrections. The first resurrection will take place before the Tribulation begins. The church will be caught up to meet the Lord in the air. The saved of the church age will rise from the dead and be caught up with living believers. After the thousand years, the second resurrection takes place. The unsaved will be resurrected to judgment. The two are at least a thousand years apart.

This passage shows the importance of studying the whole counsel of God in order to interpret the Bible properly. For example, in John 5 our Lord speaks of the resurrection and says, *"The hour is coming when all that are in the graves shall hear My voice, and some shall come forth to everlasting life and some to everlasting judgment [condemnation]."* There is no indication there of the thousand years between the resurrection of the saved and the unsaved. God is not going to raise unsaved people with saved people. At the Rapture of the church, only born-again people will be caught up to be with the Lord. The Rapture may take place at any moment. First Thessalonians 4:16-18 says that Jesus will descend from heaven and the dead in Christ shall rise first. Then we which are alive and remain will be caught up with them. The dead bodies will come out of the graves and the Lord will reunite body, soul, and spirit. We'll all be suddenly changed and be given our glorified bodies. Once we are caught up to be with the Lord, we shall be with Him forever.

After the thousand years, the Lord will call up all the unsaved, and they will be judged at the second resurrection and consigned to an eternity separated from God. Never can it be said that it will be blessed to have a part in the second resurrection, for the unsaved are going to be cast into the lake of fire.

Earth's Final Revolt

Beginning with verse 7 we have the final revolt of Satan. **"And when the thousand years are expired, Satan shall be loosed out of his prison, and shall go out to deceive the nations that are in the four quarters of the earth, Gog and Magog, to gather them together to battle: the number of whom is as the sand of the sea."** When Jesus returns to earth, the first thing He will do is judge the armies of the earth and destroy them. That will be the last of the great human wars. But it will not be the last conflict. At the end of the Millennium, Satan will be set free and will go out over the earth deceiving people. He is unchanged; fallen angels do not repent. Only to man does God grant "repentance unto life." He will find people, born during the Millennium, who have definitely rejected Christ, the One reigning over the world. People in the Millennium will bear children, and many of these children (even with Jesus reigning from Jerusalem) will not believe in Him in the sense of giving their hearts and lives to Him. And they will be ready to join the devil in his final revolt against Christ.

He will persuade them to encircle Jerusalem, the city God loves. They will seek to destroy Christ and His people. Verse 9: **"And they went up to the breadth of the earth, and compassed the camp of the saints about, and the beloved city; and fire came down from God out of heaven, and devoured them."**

Devil Cast into Lake of Fire

"And the devil that deceived them was cast into the lake of fire and brimstone, where the beast [the Antichrist] and the false prophet are, and shall be tormented [tortured] day and night forever [unto the ages of the ages]." The Antichrist and false prophet were cast into the lake of fire 1,000 years before— proof that its occupants never die. There they are endlessly tortured. And now the devil is cast in.

This verse teaches the truth of eternal existence. When God creates human beings, they live forever. The strongest Greek expression for "eternity" is "unto the ages of the ages," and it is used of the existence of God and of the saved. There is no such thing as annihilation, or being blotted out of existence. God promises believers (Ephesians 2:7) that He will show them the exceeding riches of His grace! But the lake of fire is the final destiny of Satan, and he knows it, and even today he is trying to take as many people as possible with him.

Great White Throne

In verses 11 and 12 we find the final doom of unbelievers, the wicked of earth who have not believed in the Lord. In order to have paradise, God must not only get rid of Satan, but of all unbelieving people. **"And I saw a great white throne, and Him that sat on it, from whose face the earth and the heaven fled away; and there was found no place for them."** This is the Great White Throne judgment of God. It is great because it is the seat of the Governor of the universe. It is God sitting on the throne. He who created the universe now becomes its destroyer. It is white, because of its absolute justice and purity. It is

God who is sitting on the throne, and Jesus will be doing the judging. All judgment is committed into the hands of the Son of God.

What a day it will be when an unsaved person stands before Christ, having heard the Gospel but refused to give his heart and life to Him! He will see the scars of the wounds in Christ's hands and feet and forehead. He will stand there mutely while all his life-work is read out, all the evil deeds, and his name will not be found in the Lamb's book of life. In agonizing desperation he will look to Jesus—but too late! For Jesus had plainly said, *"If you confess Me before men, I will confess you before the Father and the holy angels; but if you deny Me before men, I will deny you before the Father and the holy angels."* There is coming a day when every Christ-rejecting person would give a million worlds to have Jesus Christ stand up for him, but it will be TOO LATE. That is the day of judgment; today is the day of salvation. This unbelieving world is rushing toward God's appointed day when Christ will judge the world. An unsaved man will realize then what he could have had, but rejected, in the Lord Jesus Christ.

Only unbelievers will be there. Believers will never be judged (John 5:24); their only judgment is for works (I Corinthians 3:11-15).

Heaven and Earth Pass Away

The text says, *"From whose face the earth and the heaven fled away, and there was no place found for them."* No place for the heaven and the earth. There is a theory about renovation; that is, the renewing of the heaven and earth. But I cannot believe it. This language is too explicit. In II Peter 3, God speaks of the destruction of the present heaven and earth. We live on a fireball. This earth contains its own explosives. Someday it is going to explode. God is going to destroy the present heaven and earth, and create new heavens and earth wherein will dwell nothing but righteousness. Second Peter 3:10 tells us that the Lord will come as a thief in the night, when the present heavens and earth will pass away with a thunderous crash and the elements will melt with fervent heat. The earth and all of its works will be burned up! This means total destruction. The God who made them will destroy them. The present heaven and earth, stained with sin, will be completely purged. God is going to get rid of all sin because He hates it and will not tolerate it in His presence. There can never be any sin in paradise.

The Unsaved Judged

Verse 12: **"And I saw the dead, small and great, stand before God and the books were opened."** I never pass a cemetery that I don't think about it. The soul of every person who has ever lived, from Adam's time down to this moment, is *alive* today. The bodies of the unsaved are going to be raised. Their souls are coming up out of hell to be reunited with their bodies. They are going to stand before God at the Great White Throne judgment. Jesus will be their Judge. The books will be opened. God has been keeping books on the unsaved.

God doesn't write down a sinner's sins until he or she deliberately and with finality rejects the Lord Jesus Christ as Savior and Lord. Then God writes down that person's sins for future judgment. Paul said plainly in II Corinthians 5 that *"God was in Christ, reconciling the world unto Himself, NOT imputing unto them their trespasses."*

I have gone around the world looking into the faces of audiences of sinners, even as I also am a sinner. I could say to them, "God is not writing down your sins. If you will accept Jesus as your Savior, God never will write them down." But when a person resolutely rejects Christ, don't think that God doesn't know about all his sins. He writes them in a book, and those books are going to be brought out. What a day it will be when sinners stand before Christ and the books are opened, and every evil thought, word, and deed is revealed for all heaven to know! Oh, what an uncovering of everything the unsaved thought was hidden!

The Book of Life

"And another book was opened, which is the book of life" (verse 12). It is Jesus' book. In it are nothing but names—names of people who accepted Him as their Lamb, their sin-offering, their Savior. These people acknowledged their sinfulness and their need of Him. In the Old Testament, a sinner came and confessed his sin on the head of a little lamb. Its throat was cut, and it was offered in sacrifice to God as an atonement for sin. The lamb was slain in the sinner's place. God saw the faith of that person offering the lamb to Him. So also we today come as sinners and claim Jesus as our Lamb, our offering, our substitute dying for our sins. When anyone does that, his or her name is in the Book of Life of the Lamb slain from the foundation of the world.

The Book of Life is mentioned many times in the Bible, a number of times in the Revelation. It is not easy to interpret just what is meant by being written in this book. But I think that perhaps the best interpretation is that originally God has written everyone's name in the Book of Life. But He blots out the names of people who with finality refuse to come to Him through the Lord Jesus Christ.

The reason I say this is that on one occasion, when Israel had sinned, Moses said to the Lord, *"Blot me out of thy book which Thou hast written"* (Exodus 32:33). The Lord said, "I'm not going to do it, Moses. Him that sinneth against Me will I blot out of My book." Their names, already in the book, would be blotted out if there was persistent, final rejection of the Lord.

In Revelation 3:5 we find Jesus' promise to the overcomer. *"He that overcometh . . .   I will by no means blot out his name out of the book of life."* I profoundly believe that everybody's name is in the Book of Life and that God does not blot out a name until that person finally and definitely refuses to receive Jesus Christ as Savior and Lord.

This Book of Life will be brought out and the names of the unsaved will not be found in the book. Verse 12:

"And the dead were judged out of those things which were written in the books, according to their works." That is why there will be nobody there but unsaved people. Christians will never be judged. Jesus has already been judged and has paid for all of our sins with His precious blood. But twice we are told that these unsaved people will be judged according to their works.

Verse 13: "And the sea gave up the dead which were in it." One day the sea will disgorge the bodies of all the people who have been buried in it, believers at the Rapture and unbelievers 1,000 years later at the Great White Throne judgment. "And death and hell delivered up the dead which were in them." Death refers to the grave and the bodies; hell (hades), which is in the heart of the earth, refers to the souls. These are going to give up the dead in them.

The Second Death

"And they were judged, every man according to their works. And death and hell were cast into the lake of fire [which is the final hell]. This is the second death. And whosoever was not found written in the book of life was cast into the lake of fire." This is the final judgment. Jesus must get rid of the devil and ungodly men before He can bring paradise, which we will read of in the next two chapters, the final chapters of the Bible.

Chapter 21

The Beautiful Holy City

In chapters 21 and 22 we learn about the Holy City, the final home of God's redeemed. When I was first converted, I literally wore out the pages of these two chapters, because I was so taken up with my eternal dwelling place, the Holy City, my destination, my destiny. Verse 1 of chapter 21: **"And I saw a new heaven and a new earth; for the first heaven and the first earth were passed away."** There again we have a reference to the destruction of the present heaven and earth. "Passed away" here means that they were obliterated, done away with. God is going to destroy this entire universe and begin anew. Isaiah 13 tells of the destruction. Also we read of it in II Peter 3 and here in Revelation 20. **"And there was no more sea."** Much of this earth is water, but there will be no more sea. The only water we read of in the new heavens and earth will be a river flowing down the middle of God's beautiful city. How will God create a new universe? Well, how did He create this one? In Hebrews 11:3 we read, *"Through faith we understand that the worlds were framed by the Word of God, so that* *things which are seen were not made of things which do appear.*" The word "understand" means "to use the mind, to think." Anyone who uses his intelligence and sees this great universe knows that Someone made it all, Someone far greater than man, and that He made it out of nothing. He created it. And He did it with just a word, a spoken utterance! How great God is! He spoke this universe into being with just a word, and He will destroy it and create a new one with a word. We believers are continually kept by the awesome power of this God who loved us enough to give His Son for us, and He is able to do what He promised.

Holy

"And I John saw the Holy City, new Jerusalem." Abraham saw it some 2,000 years before Christ. When God showed it to him, he was so enthralled and had such faith in God's promise to bring him there that he lost all desire for the cities and countries of earth, even the Holy Land, and he steadfastly looked for the *"city which hath foundations,"* the city that God Himself laid out for those who love Him (Hebrews 11:10).

Like Abraham, a great multitude of Old Testament believers saw it. They believed God's promises, persuaded that they were really true. So they embraced them and admitted that they were a people who did not belong to earth and time, but were foreigners on this earth. Their true citizenship was in a better world, not sinful like this one but heavenly. They desired God and heaven more than the things of earth and time. God was pleased with their faith, and *"He prepared for them a city"* (Hebrews 11:16).

Isaiah, more than 600 years before Christ, saw the Holy City. God said to the people of his day, *"Behold, I create new heavens and a new earth; and the former shall not be remembered nor come into mind. But be ye glad and rejoice forever in that which I create; for behold, I create Jerusalem a rejoicing and her people a joy"* (Isaiah 65:17,18).

Paul saw it. He reminded the people of his day that

the present, earthly Jerusalem, with all her people, is in bondage. But the Jerusalem above is free (Galatians 4:26), and those who believe are set free from the trials of earth and time forever.

Then the apostle John on Patmos saw it. It was so glorious, as God revealed it to him by the Spirit, that he was overwhelmed and tried to worship the angel that showed it to him.

Today, do we believers keep before us the promise of the Holy City? Let's rejoice in God's plan, that in Christ He will eventually bring us to the Holy City. We too, like believers of old, live as strangers and pilgrims on earth, with eyes fixed on the Holy City, the new Jerusalem, where we shall live with God and Christ and the Holy Spirit and the saved forever.

God's city will be *holy*. He will not tolerate in it anything that is destructive or sinful or obnoxious to Himself. If Atlanta were to be turned into a holy city right now, multiplied thousands of people would leave. A battle is going on in this city relative to pornography, vice, and other such evils. You can be sure that there won't be any sin in the City of God.

New

It is also called a *new* city. It will be eternally new, the new Jerusalem. I used to think that Miami was the most beautiful city I had ever seen. Then I traveled around the world, and I have to say now that perhaps Rio de Janeiro is the most beautiful city. But, friends, all of the beautiful cities of earth become old. Miami isn't what it used to be; some areas have deteriorated. Everything in this world becomes old. You buy a new house and it's soon old. You buy a new car, and it's soon old. You buy a new suit, and before long it's old. Even life itself goes by quickly and we are soon old. But nothing will ever become old in the City of God, the new Jerusalem.

Beautiful

"Coming down from God out of heaven, prepared as a bride adorned for her husband." The city is not only holy and new, but is *beautiful,* like a bride prepared to meet her husband on her wedding day. But an earthly bride can never hope to be as beautiful as the Church upon meeting the Lord, her Bridegroom. The human mind is not adequate to describe the beauty that will be revealed. It is best described by the Spirit through Paul, when in rapture he said that Christ loved the church and gave Himself for it, and cleansed it, so that He might *"present it to Himself a glorious church, not having spot nor wrinkle, or any such thing, but that she should be holy and without blemish"* (Ephesians 5:25-27). The church (all born-again Christians) is called the Bride of Christ. Here the city, the new Jerusalem, is called a bride. Christ is preparing a beautiful city just for His people.

Spiritual

It is also a *spiritual* city. Verse 3: **"And I heard a great voice out of heaven saying, Behold, the tabernacle of God is with men, and He will dwell with them, and they shall be His people, and God Himself shall be with them, and be their God."** What a time it is going to be when we are in that city with God Himself! We'll live with God. We'll have fellowship with God.

I remember when I first read through the Bible. I had just been born again, and I picked up the Bible and began to read through it. I came to the place in the Old Testament where God spoke to the people of Israel and led them by a pillar of cloud by day and a pillar of fire by night. I thought, what a wonderful thing to have been so close to God! How wonderful that Moses was in the very presence of God in the mount and came down from that experience with his face shining like the sun! Beloved, think of it—we are going to live with God! What will it be like to live in that Holy City with God? Well, we will certainly have to be changed in order to do that. Many people don't want God around at all, let alone live with Him. If we really want God, we must have the nature of God. To live with somebody, you must love that person. And to live with God, we must love God. That involves change—the new birth.

Tearless

Verse 4: **"And God shall wipe away all tears from their eyes."** The Holy City will be a *tearless* city. Yesterday our loved ones came for a little visit, and they wanted to go to a shopping mall. So we went, and as we were walking around we suddenly saw a man and his wife approaching us, pushing a cart with a little girl in it. When I looked at the child the second time, tears came to my eyes. We all had to look away. The child's little arms were all twisted, and her head was drawn over to one side—an afflicted child. All over this world people are afflicted, suffering physical, mental, and spiritual anguish. But someday God is going to wipe away all tears. I want to go and live in that tearless city, don't you?

Deathless

It will be a *deathless* city. Verse 4: **"There shall be no more death."** I never get used to death. It is a blot on the human race. God is going to wipe it out. One of my friends was talking over the telephone while her husband was outside working on the car, cleaning it with a vacuum. She had been hearing the vacuum, but suddenly it stopped. Even though she was in conversation, she sensed something was wrong, and she quickly excused herself and went out to see about her husband. He had had a heart attack and had fallen forward, his body sprawled halfway inside the car and halfway out. Death hit him suddenly. She is having a difficult time adjusting to that death. She told me, "Last Sunday we were returning from church. I don't know why I did it, but I'll always be glad I did. I just reached over and touched him on the shoulder and said, 'Honey, I just want you to know that I love you.' I'm so glad I told him that. I didn't know he would be gone the next day." Beloved, we'd better tell our loved ones how much we love them now, because they may go at any time.

I want to go to the Holy City where I'll never have to preach another funeral sermon. No emaciated, twisted bodies. Nobody gasping for breath. No oxygen tents. No wasting away with terminal cancer. I've seen so much of it. Blessed be His name, we are going to a deathless city where there is **"neither sorrow nor crying."**

Painless

It will be a *painless* city. **"Neither shall there be any more pain, for the former things are passed away."** For many years Dr. Barrows, a cardiologist, lived next door to us. He decided to give up his practice and go into teaching, and when he gave it up, some friends gathered together for a party in his honor and invited me to come and say a few words. It was a beautiful occasion on a Saturday afternoon. They had a caterer come in, and when we were through eating someone said, "Okay, Preacher, you're on!" I stood up, and after a moment of greeting I read this Scripture: *"There shall be no more pain in the city of God."* I said, "I feel sorry for you doctors, because you are going to be out of business. There's not going to be any pain." One of them interrupted me and said, "That's all right. We'll be glad." Then he added, "You're going to be out of business too!"

God Speaks

Verse 5: **"And He [God the Father] said, Behold, I am making all things new."** That is a key verse. Sometimes people wonder, "God, why don't You do something about death, and sickness, and sorrow, and war, and all the agony in the world?" God says, "I am. I am making all things new." That is what the entire Book of the Revelation is telling us! The day is coming when we will move into a new world, a new city.

"And He said unto me, Write: for these words are true and faithful." God says, "Christian, you can count on Me. I am faithful and true. What I am telling you is the truth. Just believe Me."

Verse 6: **"And He said unto me, It is done. I am Alpha and Omega, the beginning and the end.**

I will give unto him that is athirst of the fountain of the water of life freely." He didn't say, "I will give him the water of life." You will find that elsewhere. He said, "I will give him the fountain." That little woman at the well (in John 4) came to get a bucketful of water and walked away with a fountain in her heart. That's beautiful. Do you know who the fountain is? God Himself! *"With Thee,"* said the psalmist, *"is the fountain of life."*

Wonder of wonders, God comes to me and says, "Jess Hendley, you're a poor lost sinner, but I love you. And if you will just believe in Me, trust Me, love Me, I'll come into your heart and make you over again so that you can come and live with Me in My big house forever." That's what salvation is. "Love so amazing, so divine, demands my soul, my life, my all!"

Now verse 7: **"He that overcometh shall inherit all things; and I will be his God, and he shall be My son."** Beloved, if you are a Christian, you may not have a nickel in your pocket, but you are rich beyond words if you have God, because you will inherit everything that God has. *"Heirs of God and joint-heirs with Jesus Christ"* (Romans 8:17). We are just beggars in ourselves, but God has given us all spiritual riches in Christ Jesus!

People Who Will Not Be There

Verse 8: **"But the fearful, and unbelieving, and the abominable, and murderers, and whoremongers, and sorcerers, and idolaters, and all liars, shall have their part in the lake which burneth with fire and brimstone: which is the second death."** One reason I want to live in the Holy City is that certain people will not be there. Don't misunderstand me. I love people. I have given my life trying to help people get to the Holy City. But if they will not change, I am glad that certain people will not be there.

"But the fearful" (cowards afraid to stand up for Christ in the home, in the business world, at school, on the street, anywhere and everywhere), **and unbeliev-**

ing (people who do not believe in Christ with a confidence, faith, loyalty that witnesses for Him), **and the abominable** (doing things God hates), **and murderers** (killers, walking our streets, many times unapprehended, but God knows them), **and whore-mongers** (people living in sexual vice; all sexual activity outside of marriage is called adultery and fornication and will send people to hell if they don't repent of it, trusting Christ as Savior), **and sorcerers** (witchcraft and witches' covens are increasing all over our land), **and idolaters** (men worshiping idols instead of the living God), **and all liars** (this includes us all; children go astray from the womb, speaking lies. God says, "A lying tongue I hate"). All these **"shall have their part in the lake which burneth with fire and brimstone: which is the second death."**

Notice the eightfold category of sins. God says that if people don't repent, they cannot come into His Holy City. That doesn't mean that people who have done these things cannot come in; it refers to people who do these things and don't repent, because every one of us has committed one or more of these sins in verse 8. If that verse meant that we were automatically shut out of heaven, we'd never make it—not one of us. It refers to people who do not come to Jesus to be born again.

Description of City

Verse 9: **"And there came unto me one of the seven angels which had the seven bowls full of the seven last plagues, and talked with me, saying, Come hither, and I will show thee the bride, the Lamb's wife. And he carried me away into a great and high mountain, and showed me that great city, the holy Jerusalem, descending out of heaven from God, having the glory of God: and her light was like unto a stone most precious, even like a jasper stone, clear as crystal."** Here we read of the Bride, the Lamb's wife. In Ephesians 5 the church is called the Bride of Christ. In Revelation 19 we have the Marriage of the Lamb. Here we have the Bridal city, the new Jerusalem, called the Lamb's wife. The appearance is as the flashing brilliance of a precious stone, crystal-clear. It will be a city beautiful! And all the godly of the ages will be there.

Verse 12: **"And had a wall great and high, and had twelve gates, and at the gates twelve angels, and names written thereon, which are the names of the twelve tribes of the children of Israel."** Notice the mention of Israel. Israel is always Israel — in the Old Testament, in the Gospels, in the Epistles, right on through to the Holy City.

Verse 13: **"On the east three gates; on the north three gates; on the south three gates; and on the west three gates. And the wall of the city had twelve foundations, and in them the names of the twelve apostles of the Lamb."** These apostles, the founders of the church of the Lord Jesus — oh, what we owe to them! What we owe to all Christians who have preceded us and have kept the faith! And we must keep it for our children, so that they too may know the way to God. We must faithfully pass it on. We who believe in Christ *"are built upon the foundation of the apostles and prophets, Jesus Christ Himself being the chief cornerstone."*

Verse 15: **"And he that talked with me had a golden reed to measure the city, and the gates of it, and its wall."**

Verse 16: **"And the city lieth foursquare, and the length is as large as the breadth: and he measured the city with a reed, twelve thousand furlongs [about 1500 miles]. The length, the breadth, and the height of it are equal."**

We read in verse 17 that the city wall is 200 feet high, and in verse 18, **"The wall was of jasper; and the city was pure gold, like unto clear glass."**

Verses 19 and 20 speak of the foundation being garnished with all manner of precious stones. All sorts of brilliantly colored gems are in the foundation walls. Don't think of this as an ordinary brick or granite foundation. This city has precious foundation stones of blue, green, red, gold, yellow, violet, purple—a gorgeous array of colors. It will be beautiful, beyond words!

Verse 21: **"And the twelves gates were twelve pearls; each gate was of one pearl: and the street of the city was pure gold, as it were transparent glass."** Think of it: a giant pearl the size of an entrance gate to a city, and a street of transparent gold!

Verse 22: **"And I saw no temple therein: for the Lord God Almighty and the Lamb are the temple of it."** No church. No temple. Why? The whole city will be a temple of worship to God, the place where God lives and His people meet and worship Him forever. This troubles me a little. If a person does not love God, His Word, and His people here on earth, how could he enjoy the Holy City where all we'll do is love and serve God? This reveals the absolute necessity of the new birth, the new nature. Only the life of God in us can enter the Holy City.

Verse 23: **"And the city had no need of the sun, neither the moon, to shine in it: for the glory of God did lighten it, and the Lamb is the light thereof."** Jesus Christ will be the illumination. On the Mount of Transfiguration He let shine through Himself the glory that He had had with the Father before the world was, and it was so bright that it shone through His garments like flashes of lightning! Beloved friends, Jesus Christ will be the sun of the City of God. You and I cannot now imagine the glory of our blessed Lord. We'll have to be in our glorified bodies to be able to take it.

Verses 24 and 25: **"And the nations of them which are saved shall walk in the light of it: and the kings of the earth do bring their glory and honor into it. And the gates of it shall not be shut at all by day: for there shall be no night there."** Only the good and godly will go into the Holy City. The sun, moon, stars, the entire solar system will have been destroyed. God's promise in Genesis 8:22 will have been fulfilled and the constant interchange of day and night that God created in the beginning (Genesis 1:16-18) will cease. Peter speaks of eternal day, a day that will dawn but will have no sunset, an endless day, the day of eternity! No night there; nighttime on earth is a time of danger and fear.

Cannot Enter City

Verse 27: **"And there shall in no wise enter into it anything that defileth [that which makes foul or dirty, or pollutes], and neither whatsoever worketh abomination [loathing or abhorrent to God], or maketh a lie [deceit], but they which are written in the Lamb's book of life."** How opposite to the cities of earth and time! Compare the Holy City with the cities in which we live, and we can understand why God will destroy the cities of earth with a mighty earthquake and create a Holy City where everything will be pleasing to Him.

Chapter **22**

God's Final Invitation

Things That Will Be There

There will be *life* in the Holy City. Verse 1: **"And He showed me a pure river of water of life, clear as crystal."** People are really going to live in that city. Somebody says, "Give me liquor; that's living." Or, "Give me lust; that's living." Or, "Give me money; that's living." But a child of God doesn't say that. A child of God says, "To me, to live is Christ." In that city, life will not only be eternal, but it will have the characteristics of the life of God Himself. You can't buy this. God has to give it to you (John 4:10,14). That's what salvation is—God imparting His life to you when you by faith receive Christ into your heart as Savior and Lord. Eternal life begins here.

Perfect Government

In the Holy City there will be *perfect government* because the water of life proceeds **"out of the throne of God and of the Lamb."** This life will be gushing out of the throne of God and Christ like a mighty river that will flow endlessly and be the unfailing support of all the people of God. The throne implies government.

Jesus is mentioned with God, relative to the throne. Because our loving God and Christ rule in perfect authority and power, there could be no harm.

Satisfaction

There will be *satisfaction.* Verse 2: **"In the midst of the street of it, on either side of the river, was there the tree of life, which bore twelve manner of fruits, and yielded her fruit every month: and the leaves of the tree were for the healing [health] of the nations."** The psalmist said, *"I shall be satisfied when I awake in Thy likeness."* God gave man fruit trees in the garden for food to support life and to enjoy (Genesis 1:29). These will be no more. God will give twelve fruits, evidently one for each month (Ezekiel 47:12). "Fruits" also suggests that which is beyond average necessity, an overabundance of blessings, complete satisfaction. Fruits are pleasant and sweet to the taste. "The healing" of the nations should be translated "the health" of the nations. Health will be maintained and sustained. We are given the life of God in this world when we trust Jesus, but "the water which is life" and "the tree which is life" mean that we enter into the fullness and enjoyment of our great salvation.

Righteousness

Verse 3: **"And there shall be no more curse."** Oh, the curse of sin upon society! In the Holy City there will be no sin, no murder on the highways, no murders in the streets, no rapists, none of these horrible things that are going on all over the world today. There will be no wrong. Everything and everyone there will please God. It is the *holy* City in which nothing but righteousness shall dwell. **"The throne [government] of God and the Lamb shall be in it."**

Service

At the close of verse 3 we read, **"And His servants shall serve Him."** This book was written to the servants of God. A synonymn for a Christian is a servant.

The Bible recognizes a person who really loves God as a servant of God. To say that I love Him for dying for my sins and then not serve Him is unreasonable. In that city God will have something for you and me to do. I profoundly believe that service for God here is a prep school for glory.

Sight

Then it says, **"And they shall see His face."** How would you feel if you knew that 5 minutes from now you would be looking into God's face? The face of GOD! You and I are destined for that, friends. What will it be like when we literally, for the first time, *see God,* who loved us and saved us and gave us every breath and everything we have that is worthwhile? When this old heart stops beating, if someone says, "Where has Jess gone?" just say, "To the face of God." That's enough. God's face! I'm going Home one of these days. I'll look into the face of God, this God we've been serving, and walking with, and studying about for all these years. What unspeakable joy! How can I, a poor sinner, look into the face of God? Because the blood of Jesus has wiped out every sin and stain. What God denied to Moses—the sight of His face—He will grant to all in the Holy City. The pure in heart see God now, in Spirit. Moses endured, as seeing Him who is invisible. But in the Holy City we shall literally see His face. What a destiny!

"His name shall be in their foreheads." YAHWEH, the name of God. The Antichrist has his *mark* in the foreheads or hands of his followers, but God has His *name* in the foreheads of His own. That means possession. That means He wants me. God brands me. It means, "Jess, you belong to Me." Such love overwhelms me! You can't buy that with money. The only way you can get it is through the blood of the Lord Jesus Christ. To be loved by a human being is wonderful—wife, husband, daughter, son, friend—but to be loved by God and to belong to Him is joy unspeakable!

Verse 5: **"And there shall be no night there; and**

they need no candle, neither light of the sun; for the Lord God giveth them light: [we had that in 21:23,25] **And they shall reign forever and ever."** What are we going to do throughout eternity? We shall reign and live like kings. There will be no need for welfare. There will be no unemployment, nobody hungry, nobody in need. We are going to live like kings throughout the ages of eternity, all because of the Lord Jesus Christ.

When the angel gave the revelation to John (verses 6-8), John's reaction was that he fell down at the angel's feet and started to worship. But the angel said, **"Don't do it. For I am your fellow servant and a brother and of them that keep the sayings of this book. Worship God."** So hold up your head—you are somebody in God's sight. Here is an angel who says, "I am your fellow servant," and he says in verse 10, **"Seal not the sayings of the prophecy of this book."**

Character Permanent

In verse 11 we see a very solemn thing. Eternal destiny is according to character. **"He that is unjust, let him be unjust still: and he which is filthy, let him be filthy still: and he that is righteous, let him be righteous still: and he that is holy, let him be holy still."** This means that what we are in character when we go into eternity we will be forever. There is nothing on the other side that will change us. We are fixed forever—unrighteous or righteous, filthy or holy. Friends, we must be saved *now.* We must be changed *now.* We must be born again *now.* We must have God's nature *now.* A saved man cannot go to hell because he doesn't have the nature of hell. An unsaved man cannot go to heaven because he doesn't have the nature of heaven. If a drunkard found himself in a gospel meeting, he'd say, "Let me out of here!" If a Christian were to find himself in a drunken crowd, he'd say, "Let me out of here!" Nature goes to nature. Jesus said, "Marvel not that I say unto you, Ye must be born again" (John 3:7). A person must have the nature of

God before entering eternity. God gives the new nature when Christ is received into the heart as Savior and Lord.

Christ's Loving Reminder

In verse 12 Jesus says, **"Behold, I come quickly."** It is as though He is saying to us, "Don't forget Me. Remember Me." We have pictures at home of our loved ones. We don't want to forget them in any way. And our Lord says three times here, **"Behold, I am coming quickly."** He adds, **"And My reward is with Me, to give every man"**—according to his faith? No, **"according as his work shall be."** Jesus will reward according to our works. Salvation is by faith, but rewards are according to works. Our Lord expects every saved person to serve Him. He is observing what we do and is writing it down in His book. There will be a reward for you, friends, according to your service for Him. In heaven, every believer's work shall be manifested, tested, and rewarded (I Corinthians 3:13-15).

Verse 13: **"I am Alpha and Omega, the beginning and the end, the first and the last."** This is Jesus' description of Himself that encourages our faith in Him and in His promises. He is God, and we can count on Him.

In verse 14 the Greek text reads: **"Blessed are they that wash their robes, that they may have a right to the tree of life."** How can I get into the Holy City and to that tree of life? I must wash my robes. We found out how we do that in chapter 7. To wash our robes and make them white in the blood of the Lamb, we simply come as we are, sinners, confessing our sins to the Lord and believing in Jesus Christ's blood shed on Calvary as the atonement for our sins. When we put our trust in Jesus as our Savior, God considers us clean, as white as snow. That is the way God says we can enter the City of God. "Robes" refers to life. To wash my robes is to clean up my life. I do this by trusting Jesus' blood to cleanse me from all sin (I John 1:7-9). God considers all my

filthiness to be taken away (Zechariah 3:4). God purifies our hearts by faith: we believe Him to do it for us.
Then we seek to purify our daily lives. **"Every man
that hath this hope** (of seeing Jesus at His appearing)
purifieth himself, even as He is pure" (I John 3:3).

Outside—Cannot Enter

Verse 15: **"Outside are dogs."** This doesn't mean
four-footed dogs; it means two-footed people. There are
certain people that God calls dogs. They are people who
live without God and without Christ, living only for
this world, never thankful to God for all the good
things of life and especially for His Son who died for
their salvation. A man who doesn't honor God and
Christ, after all They have done for us, is living like an
unintelligent animal. God has given him reasoning
abilities, which if he uses will bring him to the cross, to
receive Christ and come into fellowship with God. Dogs
don't have intelligence like this. So, people who turn
down all the evidences of God and His love are living
like animals incapable of reasoning.

**"And sorcerers [those who dabble in spiritism],
and whoremongers [sexual vice], and murderers,
and idolaters, and whosoever loveth and maketh a
lie."** Such people will not be in the Holy City Notice, it
is Jesus speaking about these things.

Jesus' Words

Verse 16: **"I Jesus."** He didn't say, "I God." Jesus is
His human name, which means "Savior." **"I [your
Savior] have sent Mine angel to testify unto you
these things in the churches."** In other words, Jesus
wanted us to know all these things written in the
Revelation. He wanted us to know of His love, and that
if we trust in His atoning work for us at Calvary we will
someday share the Holy City with Him. "I, your Savior,
have given you this revelation of things to come." Yet
there are people who in their ignorance and willfulness
denounce and ridicule this Book of the Revelation.

"I am the root and offspring of David, and the

bright and morning star." Jesus is heir to the throne of David through the Davidic Covenant. He is the star prophesied in Numbers 24:17, the bright and morning star that heralds the coming of a new day and a new world for redeemed men. Jesus' second coming will herald the New World of paradise for the redeemed in the Holy City! One of the promises He gave to one of the churches was, "I will give you the bright and morning star" (2:28). It means, "I will give you Myself." Many people want only the things Jesus can give. The spiritual person says, "Give me Jesus Himself." Jesus does give Himself to people who love Him, sit at His feet and hear His Word, like Mary of Bethany.

God's Final Invitation

Verse 17: **"And the Spirit and the bride say, Come."** This is Jesus speaking. It is as though He said, "John, I don't want you to close the book just yet. There may be some down there who don't know that I really love them and want them to come and live with Me forever in the Holy City. So extend an invitation here. Invite them to come—anyone who wants to may come." This is the last invitation in the Bible. The Holy Spirit says, Come. And the bride, the church, says, Come.

"Let him that heareth say, Come." People who have heard the truth about Jesus and have been saved are to invite other people to come, so that they too may share the blessings of the Holy City with Jesus.

"Let him that is athirst come." That means anyone who is thirsty for God and for heaven and for the Holy City, tired of all the sin and misery and wretchedness of this world. Let them all come!

What does it mean to "come" to Jesus? It means to turn to Christ with all your heart. Romans 10:13 says, *"Whosoever shall call upon the name of the Lord [Christ] shall be saved."* Countless people have walked the aisles, joined the church, have been baptized, and are active in their churches. These things are right in their place, but if people have not in their heart *made contact with Jesus,* so that they know they have come to Him, and that He has come into their heart, they are in danger. Salvation is receiving Christ. There is a moment when you do it. Nobody can do it for you.

Minister's Wife

One night in a certain city where I was preaching, God led me to say that there are worlds of people just going through religious motions, without really having done business with Christ. On Sunday morning when I gave the invitation, a number of people came forward to receive Christ. The pastor walked over and put his arms around a very beautiful woman. He said, "Ladies and gentlemen, most of you know that this is my wife. I would have thought that if anybody in this city was a born-again Christian, it was my wife. But she came this morning and told me, 'I have never called on Jesus. I joined the church because my mother, my Sunday School teacher, the pastor, and the evangelist wanted me to join. I never realized until this week that I have never in the depths of my heart reached out and contacted Jesus on my own, without coercion, asking Him to be my Savior and come into my heart. I want Him more than anything else in the world.' " With her husband at her side, she called on the Lord Jesus, made contact with Him, and received Him into her heart. She was born again that moment.

"And whosoever will [anybody who wants to], let him take the water of life freely." "Water of life" means Jesus. For in Him is life—in Him alone! *"He that has the Son has life, and He that has not the Son has not life"* (1 John 5:12).

A Warning

Then Jesus warns about people adding to or taking away from the words of this book (vv. 18,19). He wants everybody to know exactly what He said. **"I testify unto every man that hears the words of the prophecy of this book, If any man add unto these things, God shall add unto him the plagues that are written in this book: and if any man shall take away** from the words of the book of this prophecy, God shall take away his part out of the book of life, and out of the Holy City, and from the things which are written in this book."

Then in the two concluding verses of the Bible we have a promise, a prayer, and the will of God. The promise is, **"He which testifieth these things saith, Surely I am coming quickly"** (v. 20). Jesus is waiting and ready for His Father to send Him back to earth. When He was in this world, He said, "I do not know the very day nor the hour when I will return. Nobody knows that but My Father." Right now, Jesus is at the right hand of God. One of these days God will say, "Go back now, Son, and finish the job," and He will come! Suddenly! He expects us to be looking for Him.

Final Prayer

Here is the final prayer of the Bible, the prayer of the church represented by John: **"Even so, come, Lord Jesus."** John expressed it for us. If you had a loved one away from home, and that loved one said, "I don't know the exact day or hour I'll be home, but I'll call you from the airport," you'd want to keep the telephone line open. You'd want to be dressed and ready to go and meet that loved one when he called.

Final Benediction

Now notice verse 21, the very last sentence of the Bible: **"The grace of our Lord Jesus Christ be with you all. Amen."** To whom is he writing? At the very first of this book we learned that this is written to Christians, servants of the Lord, people in the church, people who are born again. God's grace is with all who are born again, people who trust in the Lamb of God and in His blood as the sacrifice for their sins. God's grace is His free, unmerited salvation. He receives us poor, undeserving sinners just by our faith in the Lord Jesus. He saves us, changes us, and gets us ready for that day when we shall see Him, be like Him, and live with Him throughout the ages of eternity!

I would like to conclude with three thoughts. (1) We need to be *ready* for Jesus' coming at any moment. (2) We need to *be sure.* (3) We need to be *serving.*

Be Ready

We never know how close we may be to eternity. I have a pastor friend 77 years of age. He has suffered with a bad heart for the past 15 years and he knows that any minute he may drop dead. He knows he is always just a heartbeat from death. We all are. I had been thinking of my wonderful, humorous friend when he called me. I said, "Boy, I've just been thinking about you." He said, "Well, I just wanted to call you this morning," and he told me about the times of prayer he and his wife have together. He said, "She prays one day and I pray the next. The other day it was my wife's turn to pray, and while she was praying I suffered a heart attack. I thought sure I was going. I said to her, 'Honey, I hate to interrupt you, but I think I'm dying.' " That's Roy. I hate to interrupt you, but I think I'm dying! She got up off her knees quickly and called the doctor and was able to do what was necessary to get through that particular crisis. But he has been living that way, on the brink of death for 15 years—heart attack after heart attack after heart attack. He said, "Jess, there's nothing to this dying business. It's just like walking into the next room. I called you this morning especially to ask you to preach my funeral service." How could this dear man of God look death in the face so calmly, so victoriously, even with holy laughter? I'll tell you. He knows that God has saved him. He knows he will be with Jesus. He knows he will have a part in the Holy City. He knows that Jesus Christ will be faithful to His promise! Beloved, that is all that matters—to be ready when our time comes.

Be Sure

Beloved, don't miss the Holy City. Don't miss it! *Make sure you are saved.* Someone may say, "How can I be sure? How can I know my name is in the Lamb's

Book of Life? I have never seen the book, and you haven't seen it either, Brother Jess." No, I haven't. But I know my name is there because this Bible is the Word of God, and this Bible says so. In John 3:16 there are seven words in the Greek that translate into seven words in English: *"Everyone believing in Him shall not perish."* Everyone believing in JESUS shall not perish. That is God's promise, and God cannot lie.

"What am I to believe about Jesus?" You are to believe that God the Father, Son, and Holy Spirit settled the question of your salvation forever when God laid over on Jesus all the sins of your life. Jesus died in your place on the cross. He took the punishment of your sins, that you might go free and never pay the penalty yourself. You are to believe what God says in Romans 10, *"If thou shalt confess with thy mouth the Lord Jesus [Jesus as Lord] and shalt believe in thine heart that God hath raised Him from the dead, thou shalt be saved"* (v. 9). And, *"whosoever shall call upon the name of the Lord shall be saved"* (v. 13). If you have truly put your faith in Jesus, trusting Him to save you (and He will, for He promised), you can be sure your name is in the Book of Life. God says that everyone who believes in Jesus *shall not perish,* but *have* everlasting life. The only condition for salvation is believing. You will eventually be in the Holy City with God forever. God's own Word is your assurance.

Be Serving

One of the greatest soul winners I have ever known in my long ministry is now 80 years of age. He may go at any moment. I visited him in the hospital the other day and found him in total victory. He knows the Lord! I said to him, "I was going through my diaries recently and found your name many times." He used to go to our meetings and talk to people about Jesus. He would go out visiting in the homes and lead people to Christ. I said, "I had a notation on one page that you led eight people to Christ on that day alone." His face lit up for joy, because next to salvation the greatest joy in the world is to win somebody else to Christ. He said, "I'm very ill, Brother Jess, but I am asking the Lord to let me live long enough to win one more soul to Him." Here is a dying man whose last desire is to lead somebody else to Jesus!

Beloved, we rejoice in the wonderful truths of God's Word. But let's remember that we are servants. Let's go out and win some souls for Christ! Bring lost people to the church services so that they may hear the Word of the Lord. I want to be ready, and I want to be serving when He comes.

Let's pray.

Lord, we wonder if there are some people who have learned of You through these messages but haven't as yet accepted Your invitation to come. May they right now lay hold of Your invitation, "Whosoever will, let him COME, and take of the water of life freely." You want to give EVERYONE salvation. If there should be anyone this moment who doesn't know that he or she is saved, help that one right now to say, "Lord Jesus, I receive you as my personal Savior." Thank You, Lord, for Your promise of eternal life, that someday we shall be with You in the Holy City. In Jesus' name we pray. Amen.

* * * * * * * * * *

If these messages have been a blessing to you, I'd like to hear from you. Just write to me, Jess Hendley, P. O. Box 90505, Atlanta, Georgia 30364.

Books by Jesse M. Hendley

HOW TO GET OUT OF THIS WORLD ALIVE
Seven Messages on Preparing for Eternity (141 Pages)

LET'S GO RIGHT NOW!
Five Messages on Walking with God (128 Pages)

THE UNFOLDING DRAMA OF BIBLE PROPHECY
What God Says About the Future (285 Pages)

THE HOLY CITY
The Eternal Home of the Redeemed (32 Pages)

GOD AS I KNOW HIM
What God is Really Like (144 Pages)

For information about how to order
Dr. Hendley's sermons,
Address your letter to:

HENDLEY BOOKS & TAPES
2689-A Mountain Industrial Blvd.
Tucker, GA 30084

Telephone:
(770) 491-1515